Cinnamon

DOM MORAES

In Cinnamon Shade

New and Selected Poems

CARCANET

First published in Great Britain in 2001 by
Carcanet Press Limited
4th Floor, Conavon Court
12–16 Blackfriars Street
Manchester M3 5BQ

The right of Dom Moraes to be identified
as the author of this work has been asserted by him in accordance
with the Copyright, Designs and Patents Act of 1988

A CIP catalogue record for this book
is available from the British Library

ISBN 1 85754 525 7

The publisher acknowledges financial assistance
from the Arts Council of England.

Set in Monotype Bembo by XL Publishing Services, Tiverton
Printed and bound in England by SRP Ltd, Exeter

Contents

From *Collected Poems 1957–1987*

From *Serendip* (1990)

New Poems

from *A Beginning* (1957)

Figures in the Landscape

'Dying is just the same as going to sleep,'
The piper whispered, 'close your eyes,'
And blew some hints and whispers on his pipe:
The children closed their eyes

And gravely wandered in a private darkness,
Imagining death to be a way of looking.
The piper seemed to listen with his eyes.
A cry from distant meadows brought them waking

And shook some birds from folds of fields and walls.
Children are birds: they chirped and flew away
Into a country peace as tall as hills.
Even their voices went away

And left an absence: glitter of his loss.
He blew a wavery quittance on the pipe,
Then honked with thumb and finger at his nose
And shuffled off to find a place to sleep.

Waking in lonely fields at break of day
He remembered a dream, looked at the sky
And wondered would a stranger come that way
To take his hand and say, I long to die.

Shyness

Ah hard hard hard to be constricted
By the lucid wills of gardens where
Roses compress the brain like blood-drops
And birdcalls ripple ripple down the air
While teacups rattle and the conversation flows.

I am too often silent
And I often think that rivers, streams, the sea
Owe their wholeness to their never being silent.
Then changing weather in November tells me
That I must only love enough to wait

Till locked locked locked with the body of the poem
I voyage past my darkness into light
By an act like the act of lovers who,
Riding through death upon each other's thighs,
Create, within their death, a life, a voice.

Moz

I saw him turn to bluster, clutch his head,
The King of Moz, his thunders launched in vain:
The ageing Queen sank back into her bed,
Making one final gesture of disdain.

She flashed her eyes and passed beyond his yells,
Dying from her Moz, country of talking trees,
To strike a happy medium somewhere else.
The King came slowly to his royal knees.

A chirping twilight fell. She lay quietly.
Priests moved their hands and lips, imploring grace.
Her emptied eyes looked up, where in the sky
Two stars resumed their long vacated place.

Wordless, I closed my heart. Now I return,
Amazed that stone endures and rivers move,
And persecute my friends with smiles to learn
Their water rates, and have they been in love.

I clench my sleep upon a thought that springs
Out of a nervous kind of fixity:
The King pacing his bedroom, touching things,
Trying vaguely to conceive eternity.

Words to a Dancer

What Corn or Fire dance do you want to join,
What drumming or what votive chanting hear,
Now that on every tree we see the sign
Of the black frost that cracks the stony year?
I hear a mad voice shouting in the mountains
After the nightingale: the fountains
Congeal, and icicles appear.

Feet of the tiger rustle in our passes.
Where mountain towns have fallen, an invader
Warms his hinged fingers in their ashes.
The radio utters warnings, and the radar
Reveals a shadow which advancing
Blots out the cities that were dancing.
And now we lack a leader.

So leave off dancing and take up your gun
Against the archaic horror with the eyes
As blank as searchlights or the monstrous sun,
And fight it in the hills, where hundreds lie.
O dancer, when beneath the brass fist's weight
Your skull fluffs out in blood, be not afraid.
O imitate the sunset as you die.

Kanheri Caves

Over these blunted, these tormented hills,
Hawks hail and wheel, glissading down the sky:
It seems this green ambiguous landscape tilts
And teeters the perspective of the eye.
Only two centuries after Christ, this cliff
Was colonized by a mild antique race,
Who left us, like a faded photograph,
Their memories that dry up in this place.

They left no ghosts. The rock alone endures.
Their drains and cisterns work: storms wrecked the stairs
Blocks are fallen: sunlight cracks those floors
And fidgets in a courtyard where a pair
Of giant Buddhas smile and wait their crash;
Then temples, audience-halls, a lonely tomb.
I touch its side. The stone's worn smooth as flesh.
A stranger dangles peaceful in that womb.

Worm he will be, if born: blink in the sun.
I'll crawl into his dark: perhaps he'll climb
Beyond the trippers to the final stone
Flat of the hillock, there to grow in Time.
Dry pubic ferns prickle the bitter sand.
Hawks in a hot concentric ecstasy
Of flight and shriek will wake his vision. And,
When the clouds lift, he'll glimpse the miles-off sea.

At Seven o' Clock

The masseur from Ceylon, whose balding head
Gives him a curious look of tenderness,
Uncurls his long crushed hands above my bed
As though he were about to preach or bless.

His poulterer's fingers pluck my queasy skin,
Shuffle along my side, and reach the thigh.
I note however that he keeps his thin
Fastidious nostrils safely turned away.

But sometimes the antarctic eyes glance down,
And the lids drop to hood a scornful flash:
A deep ironic knowledge of the thin
Or gross (but always ugly) human flesh.

Hernia, goitre and the flowering boil
Lie bare beneath his hands, for ever bare.
His fingers touch the skin: they reach the soul.
I know him in the morning for a seer.

Within my mind he is reborn as Christ:
For each blind dawn he kneads my prostrate thighs,
Thumps on my buttocks with his fist
And breathes, Arise.

Sailing to England

Fallen into a dream, I could not rise.
I am in love, and long to be unhappy.
Something within me raised her from the sea:
A delicate sad face, and stones for eyes.

Something within me mumbles words and grieves
For three swept out, while inland watchers groaned,
Humped, elbows jerking in a skein of waves
Like giant women knitting. One was drowned.

He could not swim and so he had to sink
And only floated after having died,
Clutching some weeds, and tolerant of the tide:
A happy traveller on a sea of ink.

I blot his eyes: waves rustle in the breeze.
Perhaps he's thinking. The moon will rise in blood,
Trawling her whisper across the sprawling seas
To rouse him, if he thinks. But if he's dead?

He must forget his death, I'll tell him so:
'It's nearly time for lunch,' I'll tell him, 'change:
Be careful: grin a bit: avoid her eyes:
Later go settle in the upstairs lounge

'And laugh as if you ground stones in your teeth,
Watching the sea: or simply sit alone:
Or choose the wise alternative to death:
A nap to while away the afternoon.'

Bells for William Wordsworth

Today they brought me a message: Wordsworth was dead.
'My God,' I said. 'My God. I can hardly believe it.'
'Just as you like,' they answered. 'Take it or leave it,
He has sunk into April as into the depths of a lake,
Leaving his eyes ajar in the house of his head.'
'Are you sure,' I said, 'that you haven't made a mistake?'

'Oh no,' they said, 'not a hope. We knew him too well,
A gloomy considering bloke with the nose of a preacher:
A poet in fact, with a charming affection for Nature:
Milkmaids (you know) and the shadows of clouds on the land.
His work is carefully studied in colleges still.
We shall not forget nor forgo it, while colleges stand.'

And I said, 'I grant you that Wordsworth lies chilly in Grasmere
And his bones are absolved and dissolved in the tears of the rain.
I grant he is one with the plant and the fossil again.
His flesh has gone back into soil and his eyes into stones
And the roots and shoots of a new life push each year
Through the sad rotten fragments of his bones.

'But although each Spring brings a newer death to those bones,
I have seen him risen again with the crocus in Spring.
I have turned my ear to the wind, I have heard him speaking.
I shrank from the bony sorrow in his face.
Yet still I hear those pedagogic tones
Droning away the snow, our old disgrace.'

Being Married

When I awake (he said) I shall be lonely,
O feel my loneliest ever by your side;
For I have dropped my root, and stuck: you only
Move through a night of sleep, conscious of right.
    Beloved conquering bride,
My kisses lanced your veins with veins of light.

O take my angel in your sleeping flesh.
I killed him from me, wrestling with your belly,
Wrenched to the contact and the bitter flash
Which you stir well, better than verse perhaps.
    Lost angel, now how easily
The ritual nights will come, and roots collapse.

I lost in night must hear you breathe in whispers,
Your hater now for spendthrift of my breath:
Lost in the night we fought; we rushed together
At frontiers of our miles of loneliness
    And lived, and parted at a gate
Where the last touch of lips was meant to bless.

An Ordinary Care

Visit the rumoured stranger on the stair,
Though you to find him must go round and round;
Upon the lowest landing, by a bare
Window that opens on to barer ground,
Plain in plain light, the one you seek is found.

These months of early cold, unripe November,
A slant of light, trembling, a woman's tone,
You so much loved, and wanted to remember
Against its end, or yours. But he, alone,
Keeps inward excellence of skeleton.

Then stand: say nothing: nothing you believe,
Or think you do, will he: but smile: and sigh.
Your hand, your hands in his, like blows relieve
Not helplessness or sorrow, but self-pity.
He missed, one day in Spring, his time to die.

That Was

That was an innocent country:
Warlock and dwarf, the hairy forest, dragons
Somewhere there, they said,
Though never seen, sometimes heard:
Somewhere in the hills, the hermit's cavern
Where all was forgiven.

There dying would only be the trek to sleep
Or waking through tall mirrors of a dream:
In spite of which all were afraid to die.
The golden princess had no remedy
When the dragon arrived
But to surrender to his lechery.

Opened her eyes but found herself awake
Or asleep perhaps in the same
Dream by the sleeping unsuffering lake
Where her grief as simple as dying
Pressed her body into the shape of a tear
Lying by embroidered leaves
To fade upon the handkerchiefs of water.

That tyrant was limpid.
With his iron guard of poets and his liars,
He bubbled through stone-walled halls of life
Sucking upon his tide
Like tiny coloured pebbles, chilled desires.

At a river's end
Streams gulp and sweat, expiring in the sand.

Afternoon Tea

She poured the tea. Vaguely I watched her hands.
The mask was fitted: in my wandering dream
Were boulder-broken valleys, a strange land.
Remote, astonished, I stood by a stream
Holding her hand in mine. The afternoon
Moved in my bones. Sun flecked the leaves and sand.
And she seemed fragile: but with roots in stone,
Blue-veined, the flower of a northern land.

And then things changed: and do not ask me why:
But privately and gently, as her hand
Might let mine fall, all love became a lie:
My gesture broke upon a dream beyond
Scones and my witty mouth and those chic cups
And the strange look that fussed me into rhyme:
An inarticulate wincing at the lips:
At last the key: and I came back to Time.

There to achieve a root, slowly to grow,
Is all my will. Here no one can elude
Desire, but in this city, when I go,
I'll leave a bedtime and destructive mood.
Her anger dwells there, wistful; and my drouth
Burns in the shadow country of a dream
Where her cool mouth flows backward from my mouth
And her long hands sustain a golden stream.

A Man Dreaming

I

Waking too early, in an icy bed,
Four-posted, with brass cupids perched in place,
He moved a little, and lolled up his head,
Mouth slowly puckering to a sad grimace,
From pillows white and flabby as his face.

This man, awash in sleep, had tossed all night,
Dreaming that in a meadow rough with stubble
Some strangers with long cloaks had come in sight:
Angels, who showed no trace of human trouble.
Stilt-legged and grave, each was the other's double.

Their eyes reflected light, as mirrors do,
Yet, while he blinked, he listened: like a stream
Rising through flanks of mountains from below
Their unchanging plainsong rose, filling his dream.
Then one, tall and ungainly, stooped to him.

The angel took him up in hands of fire,
Plying wings above him like a giant dove,
Till he, grown gentle and beyond desire,
Locked in his tower of bones, yet still alive,
Through terror and the fire came to love.

And so, when floated to the longed-for chamber,
To him his coming there seemed mad and late:
He could not bear to lose the holy stranger,
And pleaded that he stay, and alter fate,
Stretching his hands to one who could not wait.

The wine that he offered, cooled in snow,
His lips refused, although a lifetime thirsty.
Once he had longed for conquests: women now
Were led toward his bed, never more easy.
He was prevented by his wound, his misery.

And then he knew his dream for what it was.
At once a sexual panic swamped all pain.
An angry spasm shook him. Then he woke.
He caught his breath and rearranged his brain,
But took some time to know himself again.

II

He thought of angels as he ate his breakfast.
He thought of other whorers after vision.
The cups and saucers of his small repast
Sat glistening on the table in derision.
The lost self of his dream, restored, was cast
Through fresh awareness to an easter passion,

Not really passion, but a grave compassion,
That hurt like something freezing in his body,
Awaiting sunlight and a thaw: compassion,
Which brings us all in time to misery.
Later he raised his eyes and through the window
He saw a bald blue sky, a leaf-cold sea.

O, with the gentlest gesture known, could the waves
Drown all his life, and he be drawn through silence
Down in the light-slashed tissue of a wave
Under the driven ships and tree-spiked islands
To eddy like a flame into a grave
The octopus explores in smoking silence –

Then light rained down on him; the vision ended,
And like a saint he felt the crown that stings
Drawn from his brow. Injustice was amended.
But he, the dreamer who had known all things,
Could not remember why, or who'd descended
From the December sky, with folded wings.

Autobiography

A child, the soft-pawed sky held up my kites.
Tumultuous images rose from the mud.
My eyes like fish flickered through sunken lights
Under the poems dancing in my blood.
And from this great, this all-gate-breaking flood
My thoughts like pincers lifted tastes and sights,
My heart delved down to love, knowledge of God,
Waited the King in sandals on the heights.

But even then I was as cold as stone
Sinking among the ripples of the crowd
And now all my desire is to atone
For an unfriendly springtime, webbed in cloud.
I remember my grandmother, crescent-browed,
Falling from time, leaf-light, too much alone,
And my grandfather, who was small and proud.
Tumult of images, where have you gone?

The ageing chemist in his drawing-room, terse,
Gentle: the seas like soapsuds in the night
Seen from a ship: the moon, leprous, inverse,
Rising: the girl at Hanoi with her white
Hands and dog's eyes, dripping with amber light.
Have these things shaped me for the craft of verse?
Do they remain, giving a sad insight?
And have I changed for better or for worse?

I have grown up, I think, to live alone
To keep my old illusions, sometimes dream,
Glumly, that I am unloved and forlorn,
Run away from strangers, often seem
Unreal to myself in the pulpy warmth of a sunbeam.
I have grown up, hand on the primal bone,
Making the poem, taking the word from the stream,
Fighting the sand for speech, fighting the stone.

from *Poems* (1960)

French Lesson

Rain drones on outside like a businessman's stories
And inside I sit at your right on the sofa:
Thinking vaguely of Yeats who 'believed in the fairies'
I wonder why poets are born to tell lies.
You speak and the light quivers, lost, in your eyes.
I have death on my tongue, but no comment to offer.

So I stare at my hands, striving hard to seem calm,
But read in their lines an appalling distress,
And turn to you, trembling with some vague alarm
Half-taken last night from unquietness of sleep.
I think of the tears I have wept and shall weep.
There's a child in my body: it longs to confess.

And I roll my mind out at your feet like the painting
Of some idler who died, unremarked, in an attic:
Love, vision and hope in a rose-and-mauve blending
With a barbarous ochre to highlight despair.
And knowing when I fumble, three-quarters in tears,
My voice gains conviction, grows shyly dramatic.

A pose. One would say that. But horrible fears
Lie hidden beneath it, like rocks under sand.
My hands are two wide-eyed, two terrified deer.
Your eyes shine like mirrors. I cannot look in them.
'Je comprends, comprends tout,' you keep telling my hands.
'Mais moi je ne comprends ni toi ni moi-même.'

Words to a Boy

I cannot speak to you. Our chances
Lessen each day, I think, but you must still
Follow the lonely dancer when he dances
Over the shoulder of the farthest hill
Where boulders lie. Which king advances

Through the tumultuous plains, or what retreat
Is made through marshes, you know nothing of.
Only the scuffed grass and the dancer's feet
Can your eyes understand, for too much love
Affects the eyes, makes vision incomplete.

So you one day will lose the dancer.
He will cry out and fall, he will have passed
Beyond your question to the place of answer,
The final solitude, to find at last
Stillness of rocks and tumult of the past.

Return, with lifted hands and prophet's tongue.
Your people will not see your vision,
For they sleep under the dark angel's wing.
When you cry out to them they will not listen
Because you are ugly and no longer young.

The Climber

Once we had left the valley, dayflare
Came on the clouded mountain. 'You must climb,'
You said to me, 'while light still fills the air,
For no man ever has enough of time.'

The angels of my love rose to my eyes.
I was embarrassed to display them, so
I put dark glasses on for a disguise
And climbed away through pines, towards the snow.

I listened for a call that never came.
I dragged my body upward like a fox,
Scurfed with the snow, through shadows, over rocks,
A furtive wanderer, I said your name.

Here it is cold. I am tired. When I fell
I broke no bones, but now I fail to rise.
It is strange, this last time, why I cannot tell,
I am lucky; you are here; I see your eyes.

Darkness will fall. The peak stands white above
Our heads. Favour me with one final smile.
If I start dying in a little while,
Till I die, do not speak to me of love.

Verses for Peter Levi

A ragged scroll, the river in the grass
Unrolls. You kneel to read it. Through your bent
Head the world wanders and four seasons pass.
You rise and follow where your sorrow went.
Your light feet scarcely hurt a single frond
Of fern, my gentle friend.

The Island

I

THE BURNING

Like the birdflights migrating from the island
We flutter round and click our tongues above
The unwieldy hero pyred upon the sand

And a girl murmurs guiltily as a dove
Over the massive skull, bronze scales for eyes,
That looks upon her and ignores her love.

The sun he loved has put a wreath of flies
Around his mouth, so to renew his song
– Humming that tells us of the paradise

Where he is citizen, where long
Dew-softened grass bandages his torn feet;
Where the dragon comes to him and does no wrong.

The shore softens; the day has left its heat.
Vaguely we lift our hands, touching the pyre.
We cannot live where he lives, dumb, complete,

In a green fastness come to his desire.
We know the dragon of the island still
Treads in the mountains, coughing up its fire.

We live with that, the obsolete and evil.

II

THE COMING

We knew him by the hollow eyes and beard
And asked was he a prophet: when he said
No, we pretended that we hadn't heard.

With spider-coloured flowers we dressed his head,
Bowed clumsily to him, and then requested
That he be helpful and restore our dead

Hero to us, before the dragon wasted
The entire land. We bribed him with strong beer.
He soon agreed to do as we suggested.

We came to where the hero slept, austere
In the crude fires of noon. The women wept,
Swaying their long hair like trees. A kind of fear

Came to us all. We watched. The prophet stepped
Closer, and blinked into the sleeping eyes.
He laid his hands on. Still the hero slept.

We do not blame the prophet: he is wise
And after all a stranger, coming from
Lands where the dead, when hands are laid on, rise.

It is not like that in our island home.

The Visitor

After the sleepy throats of the first birds
Had creaked a madrigal into the sky,
A thin sun rose to separate the curds
Of sea, but my drab visitor stayed by
My bedside, and assailed me with the words
That had flailed sleep from me. Though I still fought,
Attempting flights to day, or back to sleep,
The cobwebs in his eyes, and on his coat
Moored all my life to him, till in the deep
Trenches of his dark language I was caught.

Rain followed sun: and on the wall outside
The flowers shuddered and shed sudden tears.
The room was bare: there was nowhere to hide,
Nowhere to go. He whispered in my ears,
Two shells filled with the memory of the tide:
'You are afraid. Often I've watched you run
Panting up blackened stairs, flight after flight.
On the next landing there was always one
Who made retreat. I bring your darkness light.
Meeting will happen by my changing sun.

'Name whom you seek. In me he will appear.
Call me Nijinsky, and applaud my dance.
A rugger blue, and offer me some beer.
An editor: plague me for an advance.
Or think instead the one you love is here,
Her brown eyes happy, breathless from her bike:
And very gently kiss, as once you kissed,
Or take me for your enemy, and strike
The mask I wear, and I shall not resist.
I shall be God, or anything you like.

'I shall be he whom you will never find
Except in me: I am the last pretence:
Dark angel of the world, who moves behind
Dayfall, and whispers truth to innocence,
Hurting it into tears: yet I am kind.
Acceptance sleeps in light, abandoning there
The tedious climb, the fighting in the heart.'
He paused and whispered: 'Else you must prepare

To ask what godheads or what kings depart,
And I shall answer, shadows on the stair.'

The Guardians

The guardians said: 'Wait for him if you like.
Often he comes when called, this time he may.
You will know it when the hawk, ruffling to strike
Glimpses his white coat, and forbears to slay.
If it be in his mind, he will
Come at twilight to the dark pool.'

I said, 'Since childhood I have watched for him,
Burying this head so heavy with so much
Confusion, in my hands, while the world, dim
With many twilights, spun towards his touch.
Through a child's fingers then the time of love
Flowered in his eyes, and became alive.

'Sorrow walks after love: our childhood dies.
My twenty years of fighting came to this:
The brown eyes of my love looked in my eyes,
Beautiful in farewell, at our kiss.
Her eyes like his eyes dealt so deep a wound,
Until he touch it, it will itch in wind.'

The guardians with stone flesh and faces of
Crumpled and heavy linen, stared at me.
With neither pity nor the fear of love,
Each stony hand clenched on a stony knee.
Grinding like a crushed stone, each voice said, 'Let
Time pass. Pray you are not too late.'

from *John Nobody* (1965)

After Hours

for Francis Bacon

The shadows in the bar cling to the shapes
Of lonely drinkers whose hunched shoulders touch.
One of them hides his tired eyes and weeps
Unnoticed, till the barman starts to bitch.

Finally we are not unlike the apes

A cawing cardinal is shut inside
The heart that bleeds but does not really ache.
Wandering the world, it finds nowhere to hide
Save in a bottle bought with a bad cheque.

The barman knows this, and his smile is snide

Your pale eyes watch, imperturbable spectator,
The bored and lonely drinkers at the bar
Who will not look like people till, much later,
They stagger homeward, following a sad star,

Still watched by the cold eye of a creator

Your face shows pity but does not relax.
The lights flick on along the Avenue.
In Gerrard Street a man red as a fox
Fumbles his pockets for the money to

Post off his ear inside a little box

You hear his fingers chinking over pence
And throw a fiver down for more champagne.
The wall around you is not for defence,
Not to hold out, but to hold in, the pain.

Your kindled smile turns slowly to a wince

For now the clocks drive us to a new day
More desolate than even we deserve.
We must drift out soon, for we cannot stay.
'Everyone is a drifter' you observe.

With a terrible smile you turn away.

Christmas Sonnets

for Pat St John

I

SANTA CLAUS

His sullen kinsmen, by the winter sea,
Said he was holy: then, to his surprise,
They stripped him, flayed him, tied him to a tree,
Sliced off his tongue, and burnt out both his eyes.

The trampling reindeer smelt him where he lay.
Blood dyeing his pelt, his beard white with rime,
Until he lurched erect and limped away,
Winter on winter, forward into time.

Then to new houses squat in brick he came
And heard the children's birdlike voices soar
In three soft syllables: they called his name.

The chimney shook: the children in surprise
Stared up as their invited visitor
Lifted his claws above them, holes for eyes.

II

The spraddled turkey waited for the knife
The scything holly clashed: the pleading peal
Of bells swung Christ back on a horny heel
To clutch the cross like a desired wife.

And now, pinned there, he flutters till they come,
The gross men and the women they are with,
Who kneel and take his soft flesh in their teeth,
And, chewing the holy cud, flock slowly home.

There as the golden children gather by,
Hung with chill bells, the harsh tree is displayed:
A delicate fear wets each child's eye

While the gross father, with the whisky flush
Deepening in his cheeks, prepares the blade
To pare off from the bone the warm white flesh.

Myth

Myths nest inside my head, words in my mouth.
Clap hands for dancing, they will all take flight,
A winter flight of birds hurled at the south,
The hush and flutter of wings, day into night,
Ferry me faster, wings, ferry me over
Where the benevolent king, borne from the chapel
And couched on a slow barge in the wash of the river
Is wept and sung to the sea by a northern people.

There the blond warriors shout out brief thanks
Who later shrug on mantles, straggling home,
Bunched and companionable along the banks
Past which the prostrate traveller must come.
Past tall bristly pines, past planted boulders,
The country of the bear above the snowline,
The hunter floats, head lolling on his shoulders.
Do not show me his face, it is like mine.

I would not share the ignominy of the sea,
Teeth of the shark, the nibbling of small fish.
There the carved barge is only a dead tree,
There nobody will listen to his wish,
Who raised a city, followed the red wolf
Over the mountain, and made edicts there.
Now after work he is at last himself,
Passive in loneliness, beyond despair.

I would not be passive in loneliness.
I would be breaker of horses, maker of kings.
And yet the myth is part of my own distress
And it appals me. The drift and rise of those wings,
However fast, will never ferry me over
The king they sing into sleep, but pitch me in the
Kidnapping shallows with him, till I float on the river,
Rubbish to drop like a leaf in the ditch of the sea.

Vivisection

They brought a new beast in to me today,
A creature that I could not recognize,
A glittering snowdrift, maned, with onyx eyes,
Hooves dropping in a rapid delicate way.
He passed caged rats that squealed like children, grey
Monkeys that masturbated and ate flies,

And came to me, where I sat coldly clad,
Holding the knives: before my skirts he knelt,
Nosing into my bony lap: I smelt
Semen and musk. It stirred me. No man had,
My thirty years. And I felt somehow sad.
At least I thought that was the way I felt.

Obediently he stretched out while I stropped
Blade upon blade, and while the blades were drawn
Through flesh, till in the gap which they had torn
I saw his wild heart falter, not yet stopped.

And from his gentle eyes two slow tears dropped.

In this fashion I killed my unicorn.

Melancholy Prince

for Isabella and Allen Tate

The towers of the unwashed hospital,
The black house in which everyone is sick,
Throw shadows in the courtyard where the tall
Fidgety prince still paces with his book.

Soon in the dark a stepfather will ride
His handsome mother like a randy mare.
While his dead father, on the wall outside,
Weeps, she will whimper softly, wanting more.

Dreamy, he cracks his knuckles; tries to pray:
Abandons that: reflects: awaits the dusk.
The friendly skull he saw unearthed today
Calls him by name and tells him of his task.

The hunched malignant owl starts to drop
Wry comments: but from the black house beyond,
A flaxen lady, pinching white skirts up,
Flurries through dew to take the prince's hand.

Though still he cannot fathom what he feels
Somehow he knows it has to do with death.
Bending his head to hear her, he inhales
The odour of dead fish upon her breath.

Somewhere a bell clashes: it is dark.
Under a tumid sky two stooped shapes stir.
It fascinates him how his fingers work
Crablike upon her white throat, killing her.

And as he cries 'O father, O lost root,
You wept to be avenged, and now you are'
His shaken fathers in white coats run out
Of the black house to dead Ophelia.

The Laird

Sad, sad the laden sky. It smells of tears.
Here the slight titled boy, black hair in wisps,
Stares through the bracken shattered by the deer.
He wears a skirt, and when he speaks he lisps
Loudly, as though his mouth were full of wasps.
Bitter his eyes survey the English years.

His bagpipes yelling down the glen lament
The lopped heads, plagued with lice, of barbarous kings.
Now in the passes where his fathers went
The rushing eagle fills with clashing wings
And, under, the royal lion, thundering, springs
From boulders that a thousand years have rent.

The boulders seem to quiver, rainhazed still.
The damp and thrifty acres of his home,
With sad sheep huddled between hill and hill
Remind the boy how strange he has become.
He questions the advancing dark, and some
Decayed forefather answers with an owl.

The eagle shrieks. The royal lion roars.
Sad, sad the laden sky. A bearded tree
Wags a slow head. And the boy weeps because
Even his vice is English. Homeward he
Wades the deep wind, while his grave tenantry
Donate the customary sad applause.

The Children

Nightly when foxes walk,
Owls fly, rats shriek, they wake,
Through closed eyes, to islands
Purled in a blue silence
Where the brushed sun is docile
And the flushed mothers smile
And the tall fathers stay at home all day
And nobody can die.

But when the blue eyes open
The horrors happen.

In a botched dream of tears
The open eyes watch years
Bring crowlike men to fix
Each parent down in a lead box.

Since they are dreaming this
But are not woken with a kiss
The children in fury
Besiege the cemetery.

Local History

The foreign king loomed at the bridge. His hordes
Lumbered behind him, tugging out their swords,
Rehearsing their elaborate battle yells.
On the far side of the bridge the native lords
Fingered their shields, wished they were somewhere else.

Segments of them were left to mark the place,
Some pikestuck heads, each fixed in a grimace
Designed to warn all patriots who passed by.
As for the foreign king, his hirsute face
Was marred by three small cuts and a black eye.

No young wife came to save a husband's head
For one by one each warmed the new king's bed
But some bald angels circled down to kiss
The swollen eyes so often that they bled.
Those heads had foreseen much, but never this.

They ripened, swelled, and fell into a grave
Where they lay till the day a hunted slave
Fell panting there, ear to the earth, and heard
His father thinking. On a sullen wave
He swept back to attack the lords he feared.

Twelve died that day of missiles from his sling
But he escaped, straddling an eagle's wing
The legends say (he turned to legend young),
He gathered men and killed the foreign king,
First burning out his eyeballs and his tongue.

After three years he went by poison, and
Was pitched into a ditch, covered with sand
Like a cat's excrement, forgotten soon
Except by a mad prophet of that land
Who mewed for more blood under a white moon.

It reddened fast. The ditches squelched with dead,
Each fencepost took for helmet a raw head.
Drums hailed the coming of the conquering ones.
They searched the forest when the people fled
And found what looked like trees were skeletons.

Two From Israel

I

RENDEZVOUS

for Nathan Altermann

Altermann, sipping wine, reads with a look
Of infinite patience and slight suffering.
When I approach him, he puts down his book,

Waves to the chair beside him like a king,
Then claps his hands, and an awed waiter fetches
Bread, kosher sausages, cake, a chicken's wing,

More wine, some English cigarettes, and matches.
'Eat, eat,' Altermann says, 'this is good food'.
Through the awning over us the sunlight catches

His aquiline sad head, till it seems hewed
From tombstone marble. I accept some bread.
I've lunched already, but would not seem rude.

When I refuse more, he feeds me instead,
Heaping my plate, clapping for wine, his eyes
– Expressionless inside the marble head –

Appearing not to notice how the flies
Form a black, sticky icing on the cake.
Thinking of my health now, I visualize

The Aryan snow floating, flake upon flake,
Over the ghetto wall where only fleas
Fed well, and they and hunger kept awake

Under sharp stars, those waiting for release.
Birds had their nests, but Jews nowhere to hide
When visited by vans and black police.

The shekinah rose where a people died.
A pillar of flame by night, of smoke by day.
From Europe then the starved and terrified

Flew. Now their mourner sits in this café,
Telling me how to scan a Hebrew line.
Though my attention has moved far away

His features stay marble and aquiline.
But the eternal gesture of his race
Flowing through the hands that offer bread and wine

Reveals the deep love sealed in the still face.

II

SPREE

for Yosl Bergner

Tonight I see your blue protuberant eyes
Following your angry wife, who sweeps away,
With their perpetual look of mild surprise.

'*Nu*, have another drink for luck,' you say.
I settle back to let your swift talk flow
Freer with drink through the small hours till day

Reddens the bottles in your studio,
While, still unchecked, a rapid spate of words
Explains some brush-technique I did not know.

A Polish boy, you took cadaverous birds,
Perched in a burnt-out Europe, for your text,
Then came here, but kept sympathy towards

Creatures with wings, for you chose angels next,
Though different from those flaming ones that flew
Into the Bible: yours are too perplexed

Even to fly, waifs without work to do.
Yudl reproved you once, in the Cassit:
'Your angels are not Israelis, Jew.'

No: but they are the images we meet
In every mirror: so I understand
Those helpless angels waiting in the street

For somebody to take them by the hand.
Still, hangovers won't wait, so now we walk
Past herons down the beach towards liquor land.

There's not much left to talk of: but you talk,
Waving both arms, eccentric, Yiddish, free,
In your new home where tall winged creatures stalk

Between the ancient mountains and the sea.

Hound Notes

Under the flamey shadow of a tree,
Near a field of water ploughed by evening boats
Trailing their slow sails southward to the sea
We have squatted by our fires, hearing the notes
Of the hounds dying out on the wintry sky.
O blood dropped in the fern, O dripping throats,

Red wells whose hidden source will never dry
Until men turn into some kind of tree
Rooted in ruins, leaves like hats awry
Shadowing their brows until they cannot see
But only feel the pull of spring towards
Clear sky: and feel the harsh note of the bee

And the small liquid sounds let fall by birds.
They only feel, they do not ever hear.
Bowed, with uplifted arms, wanting no words,
Their growth will be like prayer inside the ear
Of our sweet helpless god, now floundering through
Our wilderness, warning us not to fear.

Still from an unknown prey blood drops like dew.
Nobody wants roots now: none will be spared
To grow as the tree we squatted under grew.
When we have told our god he never cared
Badly will end what once was well begun
In the earliest woods of all, when the mild beasts stared

Over green fields of water at the holy sun.

The Watcher

Ochre like rust, the moss lay on the rocks.
The mountain sloped into the river. One
Day from the slope I watched a steaming fox
Towing a stream of hounds past me. The sun
Dilated, and a spire of birds declared
The kill. The sift of pads, light as a kiss,
Announced the homing of the hunters, tired.
Hiding among the rocks, I watched all this.

I watched red ants mine in the fallen skull
Till it was hollow, and a cup for dew,
The fieldmice came to sip when it was full
And furnished nightwork for the owls to do,
Which, later, furnished daywork for the ants.
In all this labour nothing went amiss.
Each cycle moved as strictly as a dance.
Hiding among the rocks, I watched all this.

Today, upon these rocks, the moss is dry.
Where is our grave? When will the mountain split?
The dancers turn so fast they blur my eye.
Years pass, and still I am not used to it.
But I must watch the hot wind tilt the skull
And the ridged mask be raised as for a kiss.
We suffer and are not made beautiful.
Hiding among the rocks, I watch all this.

Prophet

I followed desert suns
Alone, these thirty years,
A goatskin knotted round my sex,
My fodder what I found,
My shelter under rocks,
My visions in my eye
That mapped the slow wind flowing
Across the sunwashed dunes, or the
Scuffed dwarf spoor of the ant.
Once these kept me happy.

Tufted with tamarisk
The tawny dunes end
Suddenly in shadow.
The ridged rocks rise.
The known desolate land
Kisses my bare feet.
Infested by winged things
The rough hair of the sky
Teems in the sun's eye.
Kindling the dunes, the enraged
Winds beats up sand. The awkward ant
Gnaws in a dry pasture.

I have aged.

John Nobody

for Malcolm Winton

I slam the door. Outside I find the day
Unkempt and soused. My muddy shoes seek those
Tenants of me who lately moved away.
It irks me now, the other homes they chose.

It irks me now, so many lying so stiff,
Locked into rock, or smudged with mud like paint.
When graveyard shifts of wind diffuse the whiff
It would try the nostrils of any saint.

It irks me too that someone else's hands
Touch you I loved and hardly ever meet.
Rest your tired mind, for I make no demands.
Do not so much as see me in the street.

A better meeting we may have one day
When with long years and whisky I forget.
Years, but I am already on the way,
Though I decline to walk, my shoes are wet.

Buses, however, bore me – the delay!
Endless! – and you can only smoke upstairs.
The underground for me, its walls display
Advertisements with girls in brassières.

So, an attentive eye fixed on the knees
Of the young woman opposite, I go
West the best way I can, a cindery breeze
About my ears, thunder and sparks below,

West to my rendezvous, to the plush bar
Where a flushed rose, all petalled lips and scent,
Ample of breast, your sexual avatar,
Billows her new coat like a little tent.

Traffic of childhood dreams roars through my head.
A woman dancing on a windy shore,
Lifting her white arms, beckoned me to bed.
Was it then, or today, I slammed the door,

Refuge behind me, and a labyrinth
Opening under me, wet, dark and dense?
It was the winter of my seventeenth
Year when I lost what some call innocence.

Lightly that night the snow fell on Belgrade
And that time Djilas was in prison there.
The students pranced at every barricade
With rolling eyes like ponies, restless hair.

But riots in the square, shots after dark,
Scarcely disturbed her fringed eyes where she lay,
Who floated on our bed, her quilted ark,
Into a dream of landfall in the day.

Her lashes hid two rinsed bits of the sky.
Aged twelve, the German troops had noticed her.
A patient queue of sergeants formed nearby
While four men held her for the officer.

But my new playmate thinks she might enjoy
Being raped (no man has needed to before):
Venturing which, she giggles and looks coy,
Then browses, tranquil as some herbivore,

Above the leaves and fruit left in her drink.
I can't afford another, but repine
Little, and leave her here to sit and think,
And what she thinks is no concern of mine.

From Iceland now a slowly kicking wind
Trails its long legs across the northern sea,
Collapses down the Strand, and in my mind
Sets constipated windmills spinning free.

They churn! – loose images fall at my heel.
No use to me, and so I leave them there.
Last August in the Valley of Jezreel,
Homesick, I dreamt about Trafalgar Square.

But in the Square today, I dream of hawks,
Of doelike girls, the sun, endless delay,
Bullocks and Buicks, statesman like great auks,
And I grow homesick for an Indian day.

But there, last year, a moral issue rose,
I grabbed my pen and galloped to attack.
My Rosinante trod on someone's toes.
A Government frowned, and now I can't go back.

The helpful rain repeats the news, meanwhile
Scrubbing bird-relics off Lord Nelson's hat
And I go praying down my crooked mile
Like her in Belgrade, for an Ararat.

The patchwork ark that buoyed me for a year,
You at the tiller, when you left it, sank.
I know you had to think of your career.
I knew it all the while, therefore I drank.

Yet I thought, as the loving tide nosed higher
Around my neck, surely in straits like these
Verse based on you would prise me from the mire.
I was misled by old Archimedes.

No hint of light filters to the morass
Where I submerge, this afternoon, and hide.
I observe people darkly through a glass.
A spewing slot machine stands by my side.

I milk smoke from my cigarette, and puff
Inexpert rings at it, and startled, see
Through a blurred haze of whisky, smoke and love,
My friends' annealing faces rise to me.

They fade: some cubic inches of used air
Tease my imagination: I still wait,
Imprisoned in the framework of my chair
For angels: but today they hibernate.

So I must smile at mirrors when I can
For company, though without much goodwill.
The newspaper I borrow from a man
Tells me in London it is raining still,

Which means another drink would do no harm.
So to the bar for one more double Scotch.
The barman looks at me in slight alarm
And looks from me, brows lifted, at his watch.

My income and my debts remain the same.
Still, I can feed my typewriter each day.
My agent tells me that I have a name.
An audience waits, he says, for what I say.

My audience! – kempt, virtuous and strange:
Those delicate, flushed girls with eyes like stars,
So lately come from college, long to change
The creature they observe in dingy bars.

The creature they observe sways where it stands,
Lifting uncertain arms as if to bless.
Even so great a gesture of the hands
Can hardly hold so vast an emptiness.

from *Collected Poems 1957–1987*

Letter to my Mother

I

I address you only,
My lonely mother.
Where seven islands squat
In a filthy sea,
You say your rosary.
The seven hills of Rome
Loom daily over the deaths
Of the weepers in the bazaar,
Equally without hope,
In the shape of your home
Which was also on a hill.
My small prosperous grandfather
Built a house there. He died
Mourned by you, from me
Farther even than Rome.
Holy he rode to heaven.
He would be ashamed of me
Who attend to no virgins.
You are not ashamed.
In the corroding sun
You sit alone with your Church,
And the memory of the son
You have scarcely ever seen.
You pray he may be spared
For the arms of the blue wife
God raped in an orchard.
You do not understand me.
I am tidying my life
In this cold, tidy country.
I am filling a small shelf
With my books. If you should find me crying
As often when I was a child
You will know I have reason to.
I am ashamed of myself
Since I was ashamed of you.

II

Your eyes are like mine.
When I last looked in them
I saw my whole country,
A defeated dream
Hiding itself in prayers,
A population of corpses,
Of burnt bodies that cluttered
The slow, deep rivers, of
Bodies stowed into earth
Quickly before they stank
Or cooked by the sun for vultures
On a marble tower.
You pray, you do not notice
The corpses around you.
Sorrow has stopped your eye.
Your dream is desolate.
It calls me every day
But I cannot enter it.
You know I will not return.
Forgive me my trespasses.

Gardener

When they moved into the house it was winter.
In the garden a sycamore stood.
No other root nor shoot, but wild nettles
Good only for a bitter soup. He planned
Flowers around the sycamore for summer,
The great splayed rose, the military tulip,
All colours, smell of sun, himself with spade
Drinking cold beer with his wife. Spring came.
He rooted up the nettles with his hands.
He burnt them all, stamped on the clotted ash,
Tamping new seeds in, fingering stones aside.
This work he wanted, his hands came alive.
They wanted flowers to touch. But from his care
Only the tough nasturtiums came. They crawled
In sullen fire by the wall a week.
But the soil was sour, the roots went unfed.
Even they ceased to clutch, their heads fell forward.

All summer was the same. He fed the soil,
Flicking out stones, plucking the few sparse shoots.
The trapped flowers were trying to escape,
But died in their cells, and winter came.

Next year he planted early. Spring brought up
Over fussed tussocks, a green scanty surf.
Then it receded, but a tidewrack stayed
Of shrivelled leaves, shoots like dead dragonflies.
Then nettles crawled back. Now he didn't care.
His hands were useless, the earth was not his.
It did things to him, never he to it.
He watched the nettles with a little smile.

Then in the snowdrift of a summer bed
He planted himself, and a child came –
News that he knew early one winter day.
He came home dumbly from the hospital.
The garden gate was open. He went out,
Stood by the sycamore, watched the clouds moult,
Stood in the chilly and falling feathers
Under the sycamore, and not knowing why,
He felt his hands become alive, and touched
The tree's smooth body with a kind of joy,
Thinking next summer it would have new leaves.

Beldam

His brilliance hidden by the stone
Under which, awkward as an angel,
He has folded his long legs,
Beldam whose exit I lament
Attempts, as always, to escape.
Tentative spiders, his hands
Clamber upward, crumble
The clods, but stumble on the stone
And weave, impotent,
While into the graveyard
The small cobwebs of the rain
Drift out of habit.

The bald professor squelches,
Reverent, towards the spot.
He doffs his felt hat.
The rain hisses like a kettle.
He squeezes his nose. It is winter.
He scrutinizes the stone.
Splayed under it Beldam
The rider of women and horses
Who was only happy with a drink
Scratches to be let out.
The coarse unwise poet
Who was shipped to a foreign war,
Now only a wet sift of melted fingers
Soft under wet stone.

The professor sympathizes,
But resumes his hat, turns away,
Thinking of talent wasted
Past the chipped angels and the crosses
Silted over with rain.
Nearby an old peasant
Stands chipped and drab as a mountain
In a wet field, silent.

The hedges weep and creak
In the long wind from Germany
Where Beldam read history
Nearly twenty years back
And his long hair maddened the professor.
And now another professor,
Saddened, stumps fields which apocalypse
Renders no longer arable.
The peasant sniffs after turnips
With thunder in his belly.
His rainy lips spatter parables
On the tombstone under which
The melted hands of Beldam,
Requesting release, scratch.

They will hunch, maybe, and squeeze
Up through the stone, wizened,
Blackened, like spoilt cabbages
And be taken in the hands of the peasant
And be divided and be eaten.

Fitzpatrick

In the warped shack, burlap between the slats,
For three days in September
I scattered random ash
Between room and damp room.
I played patience while the maned
Sea moaned. It stank like a zoo.
The mudflats shone after dark.
Fitzpatrick did not come.

I recalled his face of a pharaoh
Or a dissolute camel, his long hands
Commanding new pyramids of words
Such as he had erected when young.
But Fitzpatrick's sharp tongue
Had swollen with drink: what had rung like an icicle
Now like a clapper with no bell
Swung: had grown adipose,
Prosing the days away.

Lights out, kelp on the shore.
Phosphorus in the bladed waves.
Heavy rats moved in the wall.
Blind footsteps shushed the sand.
A clawed hand clutched the latch.
From the dark Fitzpatrick came.

He brought his failure in his face
And darkness in his closed palms
To this last beach where the waves strike
Irregularly on rock.

He showed me his hand and went away.
He said nothing but limped away.
Moonlight on mudflats shone
And on the harsh ablutions of the sea.

Craxton

Sunlight daubs my eye.
It is spring. A snail oils the sill.
My tulips are in good repair.
A thrush hops fiercely
Up the Everest of a rockery.
All the grass leans one way.

Spring. The breeze travels
Over the pools where the carp bask,
Disturbing them with reflections.
I watch from my desk.
They are as old as I am.
Wherever my daubed eye stares
The blown fountains, the granite
Obelisks of dead gardeners,
Changing, remain the same.

It is the usual time.
A tray clashes at the door.
My man Craxton enters,
Tall in his black coat.
On the tray is the cup
He waits for me to drink.
With a huge dry thumb
He shifts the bowl of ink
Towards me. 'Master, write.'
Now he is not here.
Slowly morning leaves me.
My humped hand idles.
The shadows spread widely
From the bases of the obelisks.
In a flurry of hops the thrush
Chips the humped snail from the sill.
The wind chops down tulips.
What is this weather?
Autumn, and it is evening.

It is the usual time.
My man Craxton enters
He ripples the plush curtains
To with a noise like fire.
His huge dry hand
Bandages mine. He lifts me.
The stairs creak as we climb.

He bathes me, he dresses me
In loose silk clothes.
He bestows me in silence
Between polished sheets.
He leaves me in darkness.
Soon it will happen.
I do not want it.

It is the usual time.
My man Craxton enters.
So quietly I do not hear,
Tall in his black coat,
His huge dry hands.
Carry up to my bed
A folded napkin on a tray,
A soupspoon and a bowl of blood.

War Correspondent

This message sent over miles
Reeks of gorillas and fever.
Come back, a new war starts
At the confluence of four rivers.

With slouch hat, misplaced
Cigarettes and notes, shaky hands,
You counted the corpses on a hill
Mainly to impress your friends.

Unnerving studies of the dead
Prom the perimeters which abut
Trenches where we used to hunch
Taught us what they were about.

Codes tapped out in the dark,
Signals that the west could hear.
Windpipes whistling in the hills.
Hard words hiding fear.

Come back, the words are here.
Squatter in not your own home,
You count unwanted presents,
The good day gone.

Mission

Low cloud, the first pass
Made through morningmist, rabbitsfoot
Rubbed, bourbon sucked down
Quickly, vomit on my boots –
The kid pilot's (only his third mission).
The navigator screeching in derision.

Smoke of their breakfasts below
Like grey unfrightened wings of doves
Slowly flying up from their nests.
The kid pilot pulls on his gloves.

We have to come in low.

Red pointers on the counter come to rest.
The second pass: and people turned to smoke
Rising to us like angels from the forest.

Kinshasa

Gesticulations of the sculptured men
Fail to encumber the moist element,
Reflected frailties seen by us in bronze.

The voided friars, firstly turds on turf,
Now hunt for simulacra in the stones.
Denuded nuns hoot, abraded breasts

Blackly brassièred by a hundred hands,
Pledged founts breached, drenched forests
Wrenched by cries, partly uttered psalms,

Asking arms lopped off in liquid dark.
Memory shrinks back from the shanty drums
Heard over rivers for many miles.

Gaudy cranes dance on stilts: billed drills
Bite into bitumen for the swilled oils.
Amulets, pegged feathers, knucklebones

Hang in the starved huts of the killers.
Medicines, patented for death, beg pardons.
Elephantiasis roosts in the trees.

Gestured men, shaken in despair,
As tambourines rattled, shed obituaries.
Observed by us in the air where rotten

Swollen fungoids twist bark, and humus
Cakes tumid floors, words wait to be written,
Hammered and slaked words, not by us.

Princes

When the boarhound whelped,
The esteemed children watched,
Did not speak, through natural courtesy,
Or offer help, but only smiled.

As Nanny had told them,
Corn was the colour of their hair.
Bits of sky had fallen in their eyes.
How delicately the small fingers
Smoothed the wet heads of the whelps.

Six months after, the spidery chamber.
Laughter of the humpbacked uncle.
Moisture in the eyes of the headsman
Lifting the huge axe.

Key

Ground in the Victorian lock, stiff,
With difficulty screwed open,
To admit me to the seven mossed stairs
And the badly kept garden.

Who runs to me in memory
Through flowers destroyed by no love
But the child with brown hair and eyes,
Smudged all over with toffee?

I lick his cheeks. I bounce him in air.
Two bounces, he disappears.

Fifteen years later, he redescends,
Not as a postponed child, but a letter
Asking me for his father who now possesses
No garden, no home, not even any key.

Sea

Neap tide, last statement of dusk.
Domesticated, one half of a couple
Walks with the other by the rocks,
Revoking the beached boats.

The vituperation of gulls
Turns his mind to more odysseys,
Opium and amber rowed ashore,
Panic loosed in tossed woods,

Separate islands, wet blades
Drawn and dipped in some other time.
He marshals his rhymes and pictures.
Truly he writhes between consonants,

While her deep inhalations of dusk
Tauten and swell her blouse, armpits
Stained, redolent of herbs and musk.
Familiar flesh, it still disturbs.

His known hand on her arm cold,
Pressed between it and her leant breast,
He smells her scent, their eyes hold.
Islands come together in silence.

The later pardons of the dark.
Muted vowels he writhes between.
Gullcry heard, odours of brine
Sniffed as slow waves heave and lift.

Friends

Bedlamites concerned with no world.
Dead stepdaughters, undead sons
Nibbling at me from another country.
What cages I pace, no future
Beyond the bars and the treatment of fury.
It rains: Chinese poet, I watch the sky.
Also the gutters: dead people fall there,
Mostly more beautiful than in their lives.

They are flushed from the gutters: ah, well.

All right: I accept the pain.
Did you have to force me, in a strange place,
To accept it again and again?
There are angry options.

But over you, gathering and scattering gold, the sun.

Cave

Through cracks in its spine the rock opened,
And fell apart. Your crystal
Shattered and the cave happened.
Your silence filled me, sire: I fell.

In this cave, head in hands,
You studied silence for twenty years,
Abluting your mind from the demands
Of a language that was never yours.

Little labour, less violence.
Bits of wood were fitted, believed
Words emitted to make your silence.

Where you stood your shadow stood.
And your grave moved when you moved.
In this cave I smell your blood.

Casualties

Its quartzes lodged in pocked rock,
The unadmired element, acknowledged
Sacrifice, nudges itself off the edge,
Crumples and masses, falters, falls.

Catafalques, stripped from ditched fells,
Heavy meats of humanity, smelted
Gelatine: stench from the last trench.
Paeans to be written for the next dead.

From rubric words, the cloned friars
Blot surface pigments: better with no words.
Smile left on air, received by rocks,
Answering, unmaking, one tree behind.

Tallows kindled in fossil cups:
Windowed candles, they won't outlast
Sleep, breakfast, confrontations
With the past, limp fardels borne by hills,

Mumbled by moss, umbered and sleeked by
Gigantic emulsions of the element.
Paeans choked by screams, what epitaphs
Starting with what words? Better no words.

Forfeit to no sound, the hunkered watch,
By rusty cannon, relics used by birds,
Perambulations of the dice in dust,
Declensions of the day towards the west.

Engrams

Witness: my hands beyond tears
Freshen in your dead ducts.
After war, count medals, scars,
Dwarfs, fireflies issue edicts.

Hear: engrams through opened doors
Have slipped, moved beyond man.
The great sun on my shoulders,
Heavy as a flipped coin,

Pushes me awry down the day.
A wizened tree has its own concerns.
Speculate: who will die,
Who will remain morbid, who return?

Underfoot millions of skulls
Preserve opacity, melted turds
Make algae emerald in pools.
On the ground around me, shapes of birds.

My eye on brassières: long since
I witnessed the sworn weathers,
The swung comets: long is my reticence.
Long since I looked at the stars.

A fat dwarf who snores alone.
Mensual fireflies like dying friends.
These trite symbols I take, my own.

Listen: sounds shatter in my hands.

Visitors

The tireless persuasions of the dead
Disturb the student of the dark.
Hunched over derelict hands, they rock.
Cobwebs and pennies stop their eyes,

Dishevelled creatures, still unready
To be dead, heard only by his mood,
Casualties of a commonplace event:
The surprising conclusion of it all –

Needs for liquor, the moaning bed,
Oblivion in orchards, memories
Of smells, voices: the hand at work,
The mind at work, denying death.

Warned, they could not believe –
Clarities drawn from the known flesh:
Clutched at crosses when it came,
At hands, at the slipping world.

From earth, air, water, fire,
Hewn stone, welded words,
Coloured shapes left on canvas,
Breath from the nostrils of flutes,

The dispensation of absolutes
Disturbs the student in the dark,
Listening to the whispers in his work:
Knowing the impermanence of moon and star.

Windows

The formal opening of windows
Admits drowned epiphanies
With dawn: cries across distance
Blur to one sound, halved by sleep.

Breathe deep: your aggrieved mnemosynes
Weep in past orchards by the windows.
Agaric mildews their pink paps
In the 40D cups of their brassières.

Lost white knight in the woods!
Forever perhaps on last frontiers,
Restore in your apparelled days
A movement through continents –

(Thatches over night lodgements:
Gold, russet, black, flambeaux
Kindled, scraped matches in the dark.
Dry eyes seen in separate dawns).

Colours of absence, the bored wars,
Departures and arrivals,
Forgotten contests with insanity.
The formal opening of windows.

Absences

Smear out the last star.
No lights from the islands
Or hills. In the great square
The prolonged vowel of silence
Makes itself plainly heard.
Round the ghost of a headland
Clouds, leaves, shreds of bird
Eddy, hindering the wind.

No vigils left to keep.
No enemies left to slaughter
The rough roofs of the slopes
Loosely thatched with splayed water
Only shelter microliths and fossils.
Unwatched, the rainbows build
On the architraves of hills.
No wound left to be healed.

Nobody left to be beautiful.
No polyp admiral to sip
Blood and whisky from a skull
While fingering his warships.
Terrible relics, by tiderace
Untouched, the stromalites breathe.
Bubbles plop on the surface,
Disturbing the balance of death.

No sound would be heard if
So much silence was not heard.
Clouds scuff like sheep on the cliff.
The echoes of stones are restored.
No longer any foreshore
Nor any abyss, this
World only held together
By its variety of absences.

The Newcomers

I

At nightfall the wind limped back, unhappy
To comb the passes beyond the camp,
Still looking, like us, for a new country.
The rocky earth under the snow smelt rank
And the rain stood around us, tall and mute,
But a girl sipped frail eddies from a flute
And the dipped wick took flame in the clay lamp.

Presences filled the dark. From owl and fox,
Like midget penitents, the marmots ran,
Beating their breasts, to shelter in the rocks.
The ragged kyries of the wolves began.
The thread of flute and little eddying flame
Held the clan fast, though from the mountains came
The bellow of a beast not yet a man.

Those months we followed wind and river down,
Dwindling the mountains always, till they were
Hills, where birds whistled wetly in the dawn.
A great plain sprawled beyond the final fir.
In its orchards we heard the wind cease.
We broke fruit from the tame trees.
From a hand's cup we took sweet water.

II

Each day we came on animals and birds
Different from any we had seen before.
The unknown hairy trees followed us towards
Nightfall, then hugely stood around our fire,
Muttering like nameless warlocks, though the flame
Spat weakly up. But then our lips formed words
And we made each one harmless with a name.

So beast and tree were our familiars.
The river led us through the windless days.
The syllables of water in our ears
Taught us new words until we learnt to praise.
They blurred the mountain echoes of the past.
Only in dream we saw the nomad years
Where crows fattened where the clan passed.

The winter came to us on a light breeze.
It clambered, frail and spidery, down the plains,
Leaving cobwebs of mist on twilight trees.
In arrowhead formation, the plumed cranes
Swished through the rough clouds like a giant comb.
To the broad rivers where they held no lease
The tall white travellers countlessly came home.

Speech in the Desert

My hornless snail who feeds on ash
Though you retreat before my stare
The sticky substance of your flesh
Shines in the cave mouth where you hide
Spreadeagled like a greasy star.
Occasionally you crawl outside
Then hastily retire once more.
Unluckily you speak as well.
For I can hear you bawl for God
And when a barren desert cloud
Intrudes upon the sun, you kneel.
You are eccentric, but not proud,
And therefore not without appeal.

If you will quit your rocky shell
And sit down by me (not too near)
The midday sun may help to heal
Your various rather smelly sores
And I'll advise you now I'm here
But hush, please, while I do, because
I have helped hundreds so, my dear,
And you are hoarse with prayers which
Would not convince a frog, much less
That grumpy bearded holiness
Whom you imagine stares with such
Paternal pride at your distress.
I somehow doubt you reason much.

Still, the perversity of snails!
They squander labour in the leaves
And soon the thrushes find their trails
For on each lengthy inch of road
Slime follows them till death arrives.
Men are the same, of course. The wood
You can't see for the fish and loaves
Is sown with timber for your death.
The planted men stand in that park
Because they have no other work.
Uttering prayers, you waste your breath.
It is not pleasant in the dark.
And that is all we know of death.

Why do you squat inside that cave,
Smelling yourself and killing flies ?
There is a small town not far off
Over the salt hills where you'd find
A number of politer ways
To fondle time and calm your mind.
Admire bosoms, touch music, praise
Liquor and friendship, though of course
You'll tire, probably, of talk,
As of the other things, and wake,
Harried by headaches and remorse,
Daily to death. Still, that's not like
Smothering under stones, but flowers.

Sharp in your eyes I glimpse a scene
Not many months away, and clear.
The two squat men you sway between,
Hands splayed and wet against the sky
Seem less unhappy than you are.
Cloaked, mournful figures stand nearby.
Thunder is heavy in the air.
My smelly snail, soon to be spoiled
And thrown away, these pictures fade
But now your tallow face looks dead
Except that, suddenly turned mild,
The sunken opals in your head
Gleam with the pleasure of a child.

Rictus

I

The lonely traveller is warned
That ours is not safe territory
Since Rictus from the cave returned.

After three years' captivity
A little gnawed by rats, but still
More frightening than he used to be

When we first heard, across the hills,
The hoarse drums of his northern hordes
Cough softly, as shy people will

When introduced to strangers: towards
Our midget paradise they rode
At a slow trot, their heavy swords,

Already sticky with new blood,
Held point down for the upward slash.
Invasion this, no border raid.

Villages turned to sudden ash,
Burnt orchards, frightened unicorns.
Our warlord twitched his pale moustache.

He pondered: barricades of torn
Rose round our walls: our moats were filled.
And then we saw them: hard men: horns

Curved from their foreheads, and they smiled
With their teeth only: but their blades
Gutted our captains: on defiled

Smooth turf they flapped. Our barricades
Roared under fireballs of packed flax.
Dead men swam in the moats we made.

Our gate crashed down under the axe.
Then Rictus smiled at us, his mouth
A crescent moon of crimson wax.

We lived dependent on his words.
Inanimate, we died our lives.
Through courtyards littered with choked birds

Squat soldiers clumped, showed us their knives.
Then, grunting, lowering their horns,
Mounted our daughters and our wives.

The long nights led to dreaded dawns.
The golden tremulous sea was full
Of drowned and putrid unicorns.

A crablike hand crawled on a file
As Rictus crouched upon his chair.
His haggard face hung from its smile.

A pillow clenched to his sound ear,
He slept at noon, the shadows we
Rasped at our heels he did not hear.

The guards drugged, we came silently,
As plotted, took him with no fuss,
Hooded him, brought him out, while he

Screamed: but his soldiers, seeing him thus,
Receded quickly, as spent waves
Are sucked to sea, left him to us:

Trussed, thrust down into dark, the cave's
Mouth locked with rocks and iron bars.
Three years we lived, no longer slaves.

With orchards, unicorns, and stars.
But then he came, at night, alone,
Dressed only in tattoos and scars.

His smile was a red curve in stone,
We, trembling that he had returned,
Fell prostrate while he took the throne.

The lonely traveller is warned.

Gladiator

I

I come from a cold island,
Rivers, mist, unclipped trees.
Undership, chained after lost battle,
I was brought to this country.

Warmish, but not unpleasant.
The wine's better than at home,
The matrons tauter in the tit.
I get plenty of both, no problem.

Thrice in a year, I fight.

II

Pink paps rubbed on my scars.
Sucked off by the choicest matrons,
Oiled by the wives of Senators,
Taught death daily by my trainer,
I enter the arena alone.

The vultured visor fitted,
Leather greaves buckled to my thighs,
The round shield to my left arm,
The sword dealt to my right hand,

Forty thousand wait for me to die.
Only Caesar decides if I should live.

III

Stench of blood and scent in quenched sand
I looked up to see my opponent
Watching me, aghast, trident high
In one hand, net low in the other.
'Gareth,' I said: my elder brother
Taken before me in battle.
We gambolled like boys in the sand.
The net caught my heel. I fell,
The trident and his eyes above me.
So much sorrow in his eyes.
I cried above the crowd, 'Remember Moana,
Streaming fires on the shore, druids screaming,
We two waistdeep, swords raised from the eddy,
The Romans breaking before us?'
He lowered his trident and his eyes.
I took him. How he cried as he died.

IV

Now is the last place.
Deformed Caesar in his box,
And forty thousand more, are screaming.
I'm dreaming my blood: it's everywhere.
It's never been like this before.
Impartial the eyes and sword above me.
Dumbly I lift my eyes.

Old men, unslapped, fumble
The rotundities of lush matrons,
Whose hands knead their laps as they watch
The extent and nature of my death.

Forty thousand others are laughing, or eating
Sausage and bread: my arms move for mercy,
Looking towards Caesar: so much blood.

I can't see his face, but I see
The twist of his thumb downward.

Sinbad

Winds sniffed, the graves
Of each sea identified,
Numbered, still the tickled waves
Fumbling, toss off the dead.

Sinbad, your trips!
Diamonds clawed by vultures!
Flying over defunct countries
You need raw colours for new maps.

Old friends folding up in strange places.
New friends holding out hearts.
Bronze breasts iced in white lace:
Cold cups of kindness.

Choose your rock, seamate, stay with it.
Lose your shadow, it's of no use.
The last bronze bird puts you down,
Tidier than a horse, final.

Ashes and marred walls deface you.
Where is this wind from,
Sinbad, defining its own course?
Some of us never know home.

Merlin

I

My tomb sealed, my spirits low,
Finding me standing in his field,
A farmer offered me a penny,
Saying I'd do well as a scarecrow.

Wolfbane, hellebore, in my hair,
Arachnids in my beard,
Rags and rats my companions everywhere:
I, obese pauper with one eye.

Owls and kestrels shriek away,
The roebuck, once my ally,
Shies from the dooryard of my death.

II

I follow my shadow to the city,
Mumbling for meat, unheard by most,
Dream of my tomb, bronze cry of angels,
Odour of balsam and bears.

Sacred instruments, pediments,
Runed panels round the walls,
Symbols of the divining planets,
Wands in papyrus sheathes,
Twined round with mistletoe and holly.

By parchments that need rubrics
Colours in leather coffins sleep.

III

Lying still, I heard roots rasp,
Counted ants, felt the earth sweat,
Never regretful that I must wait
Till the call on my power came.

When it came, the earth loosened.
The great salver of my grave opened,
Offering me up: when I started to stir,
Flailing unwieldy arms about,
I cracked like a windmill in winter.

IV

Winter it was, a whitish sky
Hinting at snow, the woods leafless,
But no flair in the air of starved wolf,
Sleepy bear, or any other beast:
Only hencoops and houses round the wood:
Odour and sight of man.

Lidded for centuries under earth,
I, trained as a warlock, know its tremors.
The Pendragon said I would waken
At the worst time in the world,
Destroy it, then bring it to rest.

I am master of the holy books.
Shieldbreaker, lord of the forest.
I am Merlin. They called me. I came here.

V

Under the inflammable roof of Camelot
Arthur and I worked out wars.
His dark intellectual face
Gentle and foolish: mine
That of an elephantine cyclops.
The armoured boys tried to eavesdrop
But fell back before Arthur's eyes,
Captured castles, took pleading prisoners:
A purely human activity.

The queen was the real problem.

VI

Firmly fleshed, flushed, a spoilt child,
Armoured men sniffed like boars at her tail,
Which finally responded to Lancelot,
The most chivalrous bore of them all.
Then my power failed: Arthur went
West on a trail of despair.
Gawain was lost amidst leaves,
Others in fens and the black hills.
At Badon I survived the curved knives.
At Camlan, Arthur, unhorsed,
Fell on his back in a ditch.
His mail forced him down.
At the last, only his sword arm rose
From the wheezy ooze.

VII

Leave your body, eidolon eye.
Look at these pictures, scratched in tears:
Hags with udders, wenches with tits,
Painters, poets, apostles, lunatics,
And the great mass without any ideas
All summoned by Herne the Hunter's horn
But drawn away: so many pigments
Of body and mind, engrossed in terror
Of loss of spouse or money or house.
So little life, so little love.

VIII

At Tintagel of the black riders,
At Badon Hill, when the drums roared,
Belly to belly the people pressed,
Killing, raping, each one's eyes open,
Brutishly bothered by the other's body:
An animal bother, human, not quite love.

At nightfall, all blades dipped in one river,
The dead of both sides lay in one heap.
The crows had stopped craws.
Bile in my mouth, I ceased to speak.

He rose: sound came, song:
Women, rivers, eagles, strong hills.
Two armies crouched around one fire heard.

The nictitation of his drunken eyes
His throat, puffed out, made him seem a bird.

IX

I saw Arthur in my days.
Now a farmer tells men how to fight.
No fighter looks another in the face.

Propped up by bones, the made man,
Struck by what he can't see
Is reduced abruptly to a ruin,
An uninteresting piece of architecture.
(A cliché, Arthur: forgive me.)

X

Truly the worst time of the world.
I put forth my power, it failed.
Druid chants, burning of selected herbs,
Overtures to the sun, all unanswered.
My head aches in this air.
The good of the earth has gone.
Rivers kill their own fish.
Murdered trees scream.

Tomb sealed to me forever!
The art I drew from the Druids
No longer of any importance!
What is Merlin but a mad mendicant
Working as hodman and scarecrow
For a thicknecked oaf with foul breath?

Centuries I waited to be called.
I am now sleeping in a midden,
Bruised with kicks, the cruses of my eyes
Once filled with holy oil by Arthur.
Brimming with mucus and tears.

The Pendragon said I would never die.
This is no longer good news.

Babur

By night, Tingribirdi, the hills burned
In loops and whorls of twined fire,
Arabesques of fire in the forest
And in the valleys pools of fire.
Over and under me, liquid fire
Poured itself into all crevices,
Reddening the rocks, the fox's earth.
Embered nests were empty, the birds departed.

The tribesmen did this in peace,
Etching their fields from the ash left.
I know war, but no taken town,
Spired by flames; ever seized my eye,
Tingribirdi, like that land on fire.
Those forests, stroked by the purest element
Were turned to ashes to make life.
I have made ashes, but for death.

Miles from that place, we camped.
Reeds and a river: mosquitoes
Came at nightfall with the lamps.
The opium confection, then wine.
I heard music and I slept,
Pyramids of heads on my pillow,
Soundless flames round my flesh,
Faces, whispers, omens.

The dead in the dust.
Familiars of the field, vultures
Alate as angels on each corpse.
One, in that sleeping, seemed my son.
With a great cry I drove them away,
Awoke weeping, ate opium confection:
Drowsy afterwards, saw myself
As I am, lonely in all lands.

Now on the way to another war
I have seated myself beside the river.
Far from sweet melons and the snow
I arrange these words for you, Tingribirdi.
I have little time left for words.
My hard men fasten their helmets.
The ponies whinny in their hobbles.
Drums for departure scare the crows.

Grey burnish shows in a crow's feathers
As though He first meant to make a dove.
I wrought words before I fought wars.
Steel in those words like swords
Hurt me also: my books are where I bleed,
As when they drove me out to the badlands,
Wifeless, to echo the cry of the wolf.
Then betrayals by friends: the death of friends.

In the flames always with me
I will not burn: like a plainsman's ox
I return to the yoke of these years,
Who was healer and killer in the hills!
If you look for me, I am not here.
My writings will tell you where I am.
Tingribirdi, they point out my life like
Lines drawn in the map of my palm.

from *Serendip* (1990)

Serendip

The first man's footstep
Is stone on a hilltop.
The dead king's tooth,
Held steady in stone,
Is bereft of its body,
Now a forest stone
Celebrated on stone.
The brushwork is blurred
In the mountain cave
Of hibiscus and wasp,
But dead king, first man,
Though frozen to frieze
As they start the dance,
Retain a relevance.

I

The privileged foot rests
On the stone peak, forests
Under; the knotted sea,
A chequered net, beyond.
Dolphins trying to escape
Leap, but, stunned by sun,
Drop back to the clouded
Depths where sundered ships
Wallow in powdery shrouds.
Currents sift dead crews,
Lift the bones of a hand.
The luminous eyes look
Down from the stone peak
Of the unattained island.

II

Jungles where geometric shapes
Cease to exist; dry riverbeds
Cratered like the moon, strewn
With expended stones; slopes
Of stone; skeletal
Ridges of stone. Anthill menhirs
Chart the runestones of the moon,
Timekeeper of the tides,
Home of the hare, and those
Taught to obey the leaves.
Under stone and helianthus
Are the ossuaries of the fathers.
Gnawed by the sea, the silent
Island awaits visitors.

III

From ships beached on stone,
Bleached exiles, faces etched
By firewind, fetched their lives.
Language formed on the lip.
They settled, they bred,
Watched by eyes of the forest,
Shy behind helianthus.
They evolved codes of conduct.
With the wheel and the tool
They composed a culture:
Symbols scratched on stone
Hewn to build temples.
Thing, place, creature,
Named, therefore known.

IV

Jewels prised from stone,
Pools of blood in the palm:
Predator's bait. Elara's
Slow drums beat offshore.
Uncalm water saw boats
Sundered in seawrack; stone,
Bonecrack, blood under blade.
Six months, then the kings met.
Under trees they discussed music,
Not forgetting the allied arts,
In speech broken by silence
Within which was the word.
Not a bird spoke as they heard
Its proclamation of peace.

V

Every breath off the island
Reeks of putrescent spice,
Disseminated by winds
Troubled by constant sails.
Under, in tousled beds,
Are oysters heavy with pearl,
Phosphorescent eels, singing fish.
Beggars have ridden wishes
To the island of sirens.
South, the Sinhala; northward,
Angry descendants of Elara.
In the forest, the survivors:
Luminous eyes sealed by leaves,
Footsteps no longer privileged.

VI

Ichor of the incised trees;
Beverages packed in containers
By sullen descendants of Elara;
Processions of ivory elephants
In diminishing sizes; birthstones
In brooches; spices in bottles.
All these, sent beyond the sun
To be unshipped on cold quays
Of another island. Where deer leapt,
Where panther stepped, no forest.
Where pilgrims with lamps went
No passage left a mark:
Only the smell of pasts
Locked in a keyless dark.

VII

Parliament for an island
Bewildered with new flags.
Old grudges, latent for years,
Were nudged to hate in the north.
Components, hidden under stone,
Lodged in stodgy armalite,
Were assembled, iridescent
Compounds packed in containers.
Production increased, the cottage
Industry went national,
Aimed at a wider audience.
Some applauded the event;
But the unforeseen nature
Of the product shook parliament.

VIII

The revolutions of the island
Sent it beyond the sun,
Requiring emended horoscopes.
The shy child whom the explosion
Taught to fly, needed none.
The pensioners and their wives
Gave their lives up meekly
To grenade and to gun.
So with the other corpses,
More or less tidily disposed of,
Though not by name or profession:
Only remembered as numbers
In files that would be cremated
When their brief day was done.

EPILOGUE

Perhaps an evening waits
Beyond the ruptured bridge
Of some wrecked village, where
Pilgrims with lamps resume,
From memory, the trek.
Perhaps a night will come
When the luminous eyes return
To the summit of the peak:
When the privileged foot stamps
To a dance beyond drums.
Stone of the lamps, reborn,
Will shine from within stone,
If such an evening waits,
If such a night should come.

Footnote:
*This is a brief history of Ceylon. Adam is supposed to have left his footprint there,
on a mountain. The Buddha's tooth is preserved in a temple in Kandy. The
Veddahs were the tribal people, the original people. The Sinhalas came from India,
established dynasties and were then threatened by Tamils also coming from India.
The more recent civil war which has lasted twenty years between the Sinhalas and
the Tamils is what is described at the end of this sequence. At one point the Tamil
terrorists blew up the Sri Lankan Parliament.*

Canals

for Stephen and Natasha Spender

Constant flights towards identity
Through changing seasons:
Wars, politicians, fevers,
Birdstorms at sunfall.

Old habits change: wet counties
Accept the spade: so many graves undug.
Recognitions made in rain
Of cold faces, once forgotten.

Windless and soundless the ways,
Hazy the water.
Old men sit by canals,
Propped up only by their books.

The reflections of images,
Stagnant spoil of lost pasts
Fade as carp ripple current,
Return as the ripples fade:

Pursuit of different emotions,
Outflow and inflow, time and death.
Figures magnified by mist.
Squelch of indifferent spade.

Cycles

Spring: casual praise from others.
Phrases false on the page.
Latent summer, the beehives
Hiss and boil over in orchards.

Invaders of thatched cottages,
Taxed bees drone to a finger.
Summer will bring more orchids,
Scraps of wax and paper.

Fingers flex for the autumn:
Snails, auburn leaves, slow fires.
Recusants of lost seasons
Ignite into new postures.

Winterhoard in dead treebole.
Reckoned words, echoed
By snow, still fall of
Each separate word heard.

Ichor in stasis, accrued
Silence from others: spring.
Renewed phrases of music
From a ghost's perusal of leaves.

1668

The flux dehydrates my flesh. Common
Enough, the apothecary tells me,
On these islands, in this weather.
But he proffers no sound remedy,
Though the swamps breed so many leeches
As would bleed half London for a day.
The churches and taverns are seas away.
We are wet scarecrows, sleepy keepers
Of beslimed acres, ourselves beslimed.
Great fish leap in the beached nets.
We eat fish; our liquor tastes of fish.
The orifices of the black fishwives
Smell of too much fish, like to my stool
Which I, bowed under rain, bury
On this beach where each man is changed:
Dowry for a dupe, corpses' ransom,
Fiction of the brindled Portuguese
Whose Christ, marooned in the marshland,
Held a wry hand up in benediction.
Estuary-water and the mangrove trellis
Wrapped and obscured Him, left only
The lifted hand to bless unmapped waves,
Our graves also, if no sail come.
Our names listed in no parish, no deed
That we, forsaken, before our undoing did,
More than a hand raised from water as token.
So are we broken, so obliterated…

Footnote:
In 1667 a small party of British marines was landed on the islands of Bombay, to take possession of them. The islands formed part of the dowry brought by the Portuguese princess, Catherine de Braganza, to Charles I, the English king.

For A.G.

I

The book opened, her cleansed hands
Crinkled to crêpe on the page.
Where a clarity hovered and struck,
Her luck went, took other ways.

The numb hands, the tidied eyes,
Pieces not of sleep, but absolute
Without conclusion, without
Connection to the ends of days.

The ditch outside, caved in,
Admits impersonal powers.
Clouds threaten the small coffin
Which falling clods will obscure.

She is still inhaled through sour
Odours of the wired wreaths,
An unnoticed purity, embossed
On an excision from dusk.

The shufflings of effaced shoes
Trouble him with dust, query
The parity of the ruptured book
Stained by her cleansed hands.

II

A sound from all his countries
Ruffles him up with dank hair.
From his parapets, he watches
Rain in its downward flight.

Manifestations of the night:
The gutter chokes, an invalid.
Under the eaves, leaves drip.
The earth sips burnt water.

Recollect the earlier vigils
Of Brandeth and Montezuma.
Generations of lost eyes
Stare from a parallel time.

Entwined accomplices writhe
Slyly in the beds of slime.
The rain brings its renewals.
The grass moves on the grave.

She had only what the meek have.
Reciprocal eyes beyond time
Brood on how little she has left
The coming centuries of rain.

Laureate

The endless paper yellows down the years.
Once his empowered words, knotted for stress,
Drew his heart outward on a catch of breath
As though he felt a sudden flight of birds,
Constructed out of shreds, cohere and fly
Up from his hands, above astonished heads.
The endless papers yellow back to shreds.
When his breath catches now, the nurses come.

Ghoul at whom shapely women shriek because
He gropes them, handholds as the planet spins;
To mistresses and wives whose arms he slipped
Harmless enough now, and to younger men
A slippery plesiosaurus, now extinct
In a museum, on a plinth of verse.
From all the photographs his features are
Gnawed in the dark by unseen admirers.

The scorpion, his pet, in its glass box
Of small electric suns, scrabbles in sand,
Hones its bereaved pincers on quartz rocks
Whose static shadows mark no change of day.
It suffers in its own way till it dies.
He contemplates the brittle shards it leaves,
And as the lifted blinds deny him dark,
He thinks its little death foreshadows his.

A Sunday silence ossifies his week.
He flounders on the boundaries of words.
When interviewers ask, he does not speak.
In consequence he is considered wise.
He slumps back, too exhausted to refuse
The gelatines of blood they feed him with,
Too irritated to rebuke the nurse
Who praises him for patience, pats his cheek.

No shelf will hold his uncollected thoughts,
Which, at a tremor, may turn into air,
Unmourned by him, who cannot mourn himself.
The endless paper yellows as he yearns
For this, for that, for his dead scorpion.
The youngest nurse undresses, bends white breasts
To lend him better access, but he wakes
And stares at her blurred shape in uniform.

Some rare days, he is conscious of more care,
More fuss, more voices, why he does not know,
Though afterwards the nurses tell him why:
This death or that, he can't remember whose.
Then he is dressed and driven miles away,
And in large rooms not visited before
Must watch exquisite widows bend white breasts
Over glass boxes where his dead friends are.

Exile

Perhaps he is wholly changed:
But his attire, quartz armour,
Acquired in winter courts,
Shelters him from our summer.

Under trees, Dee's alembic
Refashions its own nature.
Stained by the putrid rivers
Of fever, his spectres come.

His glacial tower of words
Shrivels to an unkempt room.
A grimace of grief adheres
To the teeth of the spectres.

Through their eyes he sees winter,
Though at first venture he left
Pieces of his tall shadow
On the screes under Everest.

Bitterness lapses on lips
Which, one continent ago,
Puckered slowly to accept
The thin eucharists of snow.

Ghosts

Hurtful invaders; at our wet doors
The smeared clocks blurt out new syllables.
Where the birds fly, for what reasons,
Questions for the defrocked oracles.

Also the ships, in the third season,
Chafe in their slips, frot bows on walls.
Dissidence possible in these farewells
To you, whose absence has become our fault.

If the bleached scribe falters, query whose
Brutalized shadows fell at dawn, unfelt.
Whose ghosts, exorcised by liquor, burned
In escalations of a noon wind?

The obscene smile, dredged from disuse,
Glimpses itself, disappears slowly.
Geometries of bronze are fitted:
Hand to face, twilight eyes beyond tears.

And you, absent one, who made all words,
Eyes burdened by dead birds, the scribe's stylus
Dry on his thigh, summon the ships home,
Since in the fourth season ghosts will come.

Theatre

The audience may be dead; programmes
Flutter down the aisles, function ended.
Conclude in tedium, for applause is
Disallowed here, perhaps for always.

If the furies conflict, let the cup pass.
Where confrontations are, because your lids
May nictitate at suns they do not lose,
Caress, as it leaves, the compromise.

The loyalties recalled, even those failed,
Include some petulance at bygone ships.
Analysed by tears, dry lenses stare
Into a false despair, adieux unuttered.

Corrections of shape, the scraped lips
Falter at necessary commonplaces:
Dehydrated words, helpless silences.
Never such tenderness as in these.

The sad collaboration of friends,
Unfinished theatre of patchwork lives
That fall apart, not heard of after.
Such long preambles to absurd ends.

New Poems

Snails

The garden where I started
was hung with dead lichens.
Snails tethered to the walls,
it smelt like a cemetery.

Great winds passed, and wars.
Snails died in their seasons.
All the events of those years
conformed to known symmetries.

The impositions of the day,
the enervations after dark,
midsummer walks in the rain,
slowly composed my history.

Autumn, a time for snails.
I can watch myself redrawn:
blotched backs to my hands,
filigree work round my eyes.

The garden closes round me.
I neglect the habit of sleep.
Rain embosses on a window
prisms of defunct days.

My breath smells of snails,
my hairshirt of old sweat.
Where shall I walk in rain,
trying not to be troubled?

What Mother Left

Too many women share one tomb.
A curious squalor, for their bones,
carious with time, have come apart:
femurs and ribs so intermixed
God only knows which ones are whose

And mixed with them is someone else,
her fragrance, once obtained from France,
exchanged for less expensive smells.

These relics of my mother, which
came in brown paper, caused me griefs,
the rich brocades, the ornaments,
napthalene balls, dead photographs,
and a white bra, lapsed in the cups
since she last slipped it off to sleep.

Gondwana Rocks

Heavy the climbing wind,
burdened with coming rain.
At the road's edges are
black stands of conifer.
Above, anarchic rocks,
grotesque in disarray.
left by a continent
which slowly disappeared;
scoured and depleted by
a hundred million rains.

They stand in silhouette
above the windwarped pines,
more corpsed with memories than
ruins which castles leave.
Though they have stood much wear,
have endured more than grief
and survived more than war,
these rocks now bear no runes
more than those worked by wind,
great shifts of earth, and rains.

But these gnarled outcrops are
connections with what is.
The cold salacities
of night, day's fall and flare,
unending cycles, pass
at the same charted pace.
Forest on forest dies
at charted pace, beneath
the scarred rocks which maintain
a stillness not of death.

The constant wheel of stars
turns over them in time.
Glaciers, tidal waves,
sandstorms and human hands
have paused on them, then passed.
Ghosts follow other ghosts,
up climbing stairs of wind,
across black stands of pine,
to the last source of loss:
the rocks, the coming rain.

Behind the Door

A corpse puts on my clothes.
A dead man fills my shoes
with his infected feet.
My spectacles can't see.
I stand before a door
hewn out of blackened stone
to which I hold no key.

The friends I made when young
patrol the western shore.
They call me to betray
all that I have, and come.
Maybe I will, some day,
but this has tired me out,
this trip to who I am.

The ratchets of the dark
shriek, and the time arrives
for opening the door.
Time not to be afraid.
For whatever stands behind
– angel, monster or me –
took many years to find.

Inside the Cyclone

The satellite's lens focuses on the cyclone's
myopic eye, phosphorescent, miles beyond land.
Still as a millpond, riddled with whirlpool wind,
it darkens the sea, causes the sun's eclipse.
From the crumpled water the tsunami rises,
a blinded cyclops, driven by winds like whips.
The first darkness pulsates under your eyelids,
reaches your womb, chills your nipples and lips.
On the wrecked beach you watch a shroud of seabirds
flap on the flesh sucked from dissected ships.

Thousands of runaway trains sound in the roar
of the approaching cyclone under no sun.
The satellite's lens encircles you on the shore,
tearless as darkness fills you, deepbosomed one.

Tribal

Quietly I move inside
the ferned cave of the word.
Thorned stalactites of rain
crowd round me as I praise
those less unhappy days:
the stasis of the world,
when all silence, accrued,
slewed to become my name.

Glistening ferns under sun.
My sister with the full breasts,
through what architraves of dark
will it come to be once more?
My fingers at wonted work
on a treadmill of steel keys
which open no doors ever,
cover the endless paper.

The arrivals of burning ferns
conform to a strict context.
The flexed muscle of the river
sends the salmon upstream.
I rest my head on your belly,
my sister with the taut breasts.
The water becomes my body.
I smell the ashes of the sun.

Container

The aluminium container in which I hid
your poems and letters from a raging spouse,
aged, and, filled too full, burst its lid.

You remain the image of a saint who sent
flights of doves into an empty house,
and in this way you remain innocent.

Containers of love are tampered with
constantly, by curious hands which don't
know what it is to handle love or death.

Each of us must wear our lives like clothes
to be shed; years move; you don't know
much about this. I can't tell you of those

times when the mountain moves, or
how it is when you are there; what revives
in me and opens up a long shut door.

But I think I have not wasted all my lives.

From a Deaf Ear

Sounds I hear in the air, music I cannot
relate to, or separate from the other sounds
humanity perpetrates, these disappear
into my damaged ear, still undeciphered.
Clearer than any other sound I have heard
your voice was, when we wept upon our islands,
and each called to the other to come nearer.

You, when alone, can dissipate the silence
with unseen instruments and dead men's voices,
not hollowtoned, richer for your remembrance
of a young girl who sang, her moist lips parted.
With paradox implicit in your choices,
made or unmade, today you choose to travel
beyond our islands, where I cannot follow.

I hear the deep waves lapse under the window.
You, wherever you are, send me your music
as though you sang to me across the water,
the childlike notes audible to my deafness.
Whether on your morning walk through flowered trees
or after nightfall, fingering your long hair,
a gleaming harp, you send me messages
fashioned from music you can make me hear.

In this Weather

In this weather, a reversal of rain.
Palms uplifted, I approach the angel.
Actually, what was he in this weather
but silent as he was, the first time?

'I will enclose you with my wings,' he
finally said. 'My wings are around you.
Do you not know the smell of my dry
plumage, do you not realise who I am?'

I know. But I prefer the smell that she
carries in her breasts and her breath; if
I am to be carried anywhere, it should be
possibly down the river of her life.

But a human stench rises from the shore
and my shoes where they walk squelch in sand.
Runes of water are read in the desert.
Sunlight hardens the shape of a cross.

Why should I dedicate a name to these
delicately connected and precise words,
flying in a burntout afternoon, wry birds,
to where she is, not where the angel is?

As of Now

Time has passed, she hasn't come.
Once there were guns and betrayals.

In the delta, stained bodies of men
earned my typewriter a banner byline.

Once there were airplanes to adventure:
unheard rivers, unfound parts of myself,

accidentally come upon; the lost tribes,
the rescued prisoners; once there were

orchids in the mountains, and promises:
the delicate appraisals made by death.

Once the moon watched, in five continents,
my beds rumpled by women, not by love.

Now why should the absence of one woman
interpose itself between the moon and me?

Meetings in Mumbai

On Sundays, usually, I find my ghost,
bedraggled and unshaven, by my bed.
Over black coffee, evenly scarred toast,
we share the papers, but we do not speak.
All conversation now would be grotesque.
He clings like wet cloth, will not disappear.
It's not my fault that he's become so weak,
his dreadlocks white, his face in disrepair.
Mirrors provide no help, take me to task.
With bloodstained eyeballs he accuses me.
When we left London he mislaid his mask,
and, some days after that, his poetry.

Weeping, my shadow brother will not tell
from where or for what reason he has come.
He searched out coffins with no compromise,
and tried, before his due time, to reach hell.
The brittle framework that contained his eyes
fell down through small erosive sips of rum.
He's forced to wear his face, and when it cries
it twitches, a wet snail pulled from its shell,
or the spilled entrail of a butchered saint.
Him my ghost envies, once left in the lurch
by god and friends, but still preserved in paint
on the drab wall of some suburban church.

A child's rhyme told his history all the while:
the crooked mile he walked to where he is;
the crooked sixpence underneath the style.
London behind him, and his mask still lost,
he floundered in the heat, his wilderness
always within him, whom he looked at least.

Now when he looks out, under miles of blue,
upon the singing tree, shaped like a harp
responsive to the wind, the birds accrue.
Down arabesques of air they dart and chirp.
They're not original in the things they do,
but shake him now, because he did them too.

My brother's face leers at me, wornout, wan.
My shadow enemy, my ghost who grieves
each Sunday for the things he has not done.
As his drained mouth explains itself to me,
his sentences fall, soundless, like the leaves
swept up in parks, and burnt: like poetry.

Leaf

Little fugitive, you have paused between
snailcoloured boulders slimed with early mist,
left hand tilted upward from the wrist,
right hand rested on a rounded hip.
Poised for temple drumbeats from the south,
you freeze into a pose that shows your etched
profile; blown hair obscures your tender mouth.

Thrushes whistle, the inveterate dove
intones from its tree a dull lament.
My headache leads to memories of war,
of those once known, shadowless with the dead.
Immobile between rocks, green leaves surround you.
Only black hair blown back by valley winds
persuades me what I see is not a statue.

Elsewhere the knouts, monotonous, rise and fall.
The fruit, bitten into, decomposes
in the mouth. The innocent totems of evil,
uniforms and computers, rule the world.
But here, with clear weather to the west,
I watch the peak, senile since its first days,
rise up, worshipped, from the pine forest.

Accumulations of stillness and silence,
found always in mountains, also in you,
that instant you stand, sculpted by wind,
time in stasis, night not yet come.
No tears for lost love, for grief no relief
elsewhere, but here, where boulders and trees are.
grow gently in me, delicate green leaf.

The Way it Was

Slowly the world tilts over on one side,
diurnally, forgetting all its deaths,
its birthdays, anniversaries, where a war
flowered like a boil, or when. With it I turn.
Sometimes I yearn for those not fallible,
those whose neuroses are not my concern.

The diligent altars of flesh where I knelt
did not last. Incense I did not want
fumed on the stone. Chanel had made the scent.
Lace bras, wispy knickers, charred in flame.
Why do you want to know of these funeral rites?
Why do you blame me for what I was or am?

Difficult descent, and to return to what?
Once more, the trivialities, so ancient:
children, possessed or not; spouses; postures;
traumas made flesh; and I from my carapace,
have emerged for a last lonely grimace
at what I was or am, under saturnine stars.

I remember I once had that shell, my shield,
open only to you. You give me tears to sip.
Why make me shed my shell, make me yield,
return me to the horror of being human?
Why blame me now because the taste on my lips
is the taste of the tears and love of one woman?

The Rat Explains

More than a monolith, he was my God.
Smallest of lives beneath his Everest,
the morsels from his table kept me fed,
as hidden under it I watched him fast.
I fled his face. *For none that look on it*
shall live. The flaw in him was poetry.
It came, it went, it heard his step, it hid.
He couldn't find it, so he turned on me.
He was afraid of me, ashamed to fear
the flash of dirty fur across his floor.

He baited iron traps, put poison down.
I squealed and ran away, a flash of fur.
He started his fierce hatred of me then,
called up his evil angels, shut the door.
In the garden after dark he walks alone,
except for owls, waits to be made dead.
He stole my options as he took my home.
He made me starve for crimes I never did.
He grudged me scraps he did not want to eat.
In his long dying, he will atone for it.

But he, since somehow guiltless, is my God.
He grew to dread and hate me, and became
weaker than he once was, because afraid.
I've shown no mercy, made the worst of him.
He shuddered back from my polluted flesh,
which now I grind harshly against his thigh.
He never knew this place of skulls and ash,
where the steel spike is driven deep inside.
And how should he ever have understood
why I now gnaw at him, lick up his blood?

Eight Years After

Under our feet the harsh subcontinent
where you and I were born, and this will be
the seventh of your birthdays we have spent
together. Eight years we have been together.
Eight years I have inhaled whatever scent
you choose to use, and spices from your body.
Eight years I have inhabited your weather,
the clear and darker seasons of your mind.
We have been more than married. It was meant.
We've lived in each other. It was meant to be.

You have grown up over eight years to find
with a clarity you once did not possess,
when you look into yourself, who you see.
You enter and leave the doorways of stress.
You have learnt to accept what you refused
to believe before: that your ripeness of body
isn't the only reason people like you.
You've learnt it is possible to be amused
by yourself and by all the billions alive.
Eight years now. Today it is proved true.

Happy birthday, dear love. You are forty-five,
even more beautiful than when we met first.
For eight years we've travelled the same ways.
Sometimes we came on monsters in the maze
where we were lost. But we outfaced the worst.
What we found was not a question of choice,
shaped at the start by threats of loss, by tears,
now healed and made whole, so that your voice
responds to mine still, after eight years.

Once

It happens to you once and only once.
You stare into yourself for many years,
a childhood habit, followed ever since,
and then by accident the face appears
you recognize but have not ever known.

Delicate features of an ancient race,
a classic beauty chiselled from dark stone,
call back the memory of another place
you were acquainted with in other times.

From your exhausted mind the memory climbs
as after a thrown stone the water clears:
the world made flesh, her body of deep bronze
held in your arms after too many years.
It happens to you once and only once.

Disguises

Always they disguised themselves as you,
came with delicate hands, with long hair,
effervescent eyes and liquid lips
into my arms: their names escape me.

Then, once, the black rind of a brassière,
hung from a chair, destroyed my history.
The rich orchards of flesh lay wasted,
and the fruit, tasted, was thrown away.

Monastic weather before you arrived,
years too late, but I recognized you.
Mollescent lips, in an ancient rite,
claimed me, calmed me. I became yours.

The leftover pictures still unroll
to a branch in flower, you in white.
How two people turned to one person
was a good story, but it had to end.

Because you need to, you will forget
these restless years, now so much history.
But if strangers ever settle in your arms,
they will always come disguised as me.

Derelictions

Winter filled the rivers with bluewhite ice.
The currents swirled armless, depilated trees
downstream on rafts to sawmill cemeteries.
In the local diet, cheap whisky was a staple.
Men and women fell daily off the sidewalks.
The Inuit were in their time a proud people.

Northward great bears roared, stranded on floes.
Colonies of walrus and seal; penguin colonies
badly disguised as butlers. The goodness goes.
Likewise, southward, millions of humped bison,
blinded like popstars by the hair in their eyes,
blundered into bullets, made dead for no reason.

The tribes, north and south, who once fed on these
creatures, were also made dead or ashamed.
Certain animals turned into protected species.
Reservations were raised to protect once proud men.
Coins minted from minerals, paper notes from trees
kill us all, very slowly. Who can be blamed?

As children, you and I may have had some concept
of what existence was, how it might conclude.
Each of us had to be born of a father and mother,
always flawed in some fashion we could sense.
We, closer than most people are, must accept
we are flawed also. We are our own evidence.

The cycles have continued too many centuries:
collapse of the body, menopause of the mind.
We are constantly reborne, dismantled trees.
rafted on currents to be reprocessed downriver.
When what will stop my eye seals your long lashes,
our time to be with each other will be over.

We start out as white slime, and end up ashes.

Mislaid Children

In the garden your clear call
echos, unanswered. Tears start.
Where are our fictive children?
I search for them in my books.
There they are not reported.
I clasp you close to my heart
querying their absence at dawn.
Why are they not at your breast?

Because they will not be born
and will never allow us rest.

You say they would have my eyes,
my hands and my eyes. You smile
with tenderness in your face,
with sadness and tenderness.
What would they take from you?
Beauty and elegance, style,
your grace of spirit and body,
your gladness in all you do.

Wait forever and a while,
but they will not come to you.

The garden is made ready
for the eyes that will never live.
Who seek themselves in my books?
Our children, who never leave
visible spoor on the lawn.
Breasts pressed hard to my breast,
weep, for you know they are lost
whom we have never possessed.

Still we hear, far off, unborn
children weeping, uncaressed.

Weather Forecast

When I lay dying, you came to me without
premise on your part, and, to what was left
of me, no promise. But you brought a book,
and later, in those lines, I knew your face,
forty years old, with a girl's innocence:
as beautiful as the face I dreamt of once.

Afterwards when we met, how much you hid.
Somewhere in you there was a secret place,
and where your roots were terrified me most,
old ethics and new money; then I glimpsed
what you had hidden, and it was your ghost.
You were my other half, we were both dying.

I had drowned my knowledge in a bitter cup.
On the first day of a new monsoon, you came.
From the place I was lying you raised me up.
Ghost spoke to ghost, you suddenly became
entire, and knew the person you should be.
I shed my shroud, I entered my own name.

Childlike in freedom, we choose not to see.
Named for a river, you flow through my arms.
But we're still chained in cells of earlier choice,
where one false footstep will set off alarms.
We do not choose to see the black abyss,
but it may raise its dead eyes, and see us.

The Shadow Times

1

Her smell is of moist leaves,
faintly astringent, fresh,
and sometimes, should she wake
from sleep, of newbaked loaves.
Sunlight flows through her days
and the substance of her flesh,
yielding and smooth, is like
honey dripped from the comb.
Her spittle tastes of cloves.
She's taught me how to praise.
But when her shadows mesh
in her, she has no home.

2

She's restless when she rests.
Her fists clench as she sleeps.
Her mouth is twitched by stress.
She says no words, but weeps
soundlessly, heaves her breasts,
then gasps, and her body shakes.
Called back from a wilderness
walked without will, she wakes.
She's met old griefs made new,
though she slept tightly curled.
All a child's dreads came true
in worlds within her world.

3

With liquid lips and eyes,
and nightfall in her head,
she carries in her clothes
breasts heavy as twin doves.
They flutter when she moves.
Her beauty's made her wise.
She's read what writers said.
The language that she chose
she's learnt alone for years.
But then the shadows come
to drain her, leave her dumb
humbled, once more in tears.

4

She's hidden from the world
by the same night she fears,
and still when wakened first
she shudders from a choice.
Child left in a charred maze,
she wastes too many tears.
Her words are wisps uncurled
from lips that have no voice.
Light will implode her days,
the shadow times that were,
like dancers, be dispersed
and language answer her.

Body

Body made of music, of different
colours, pale caramel, or where gold suns
breathed on it harder, golden, or deep bronze,
though much depends which way the light has leant,
or with what brilliance the moon enters
your huge fringed eyes and your cascaded hair.
Body of different textures and contours:
the queenly breasts, the smooth sweep of the belly,
the almost liquid softness of the bare
flesh in the curve down to the hooded valley.
Body of different odours: of French scent,
of thyme and earth after the rain has started:
a fragrance both wanton and innocent,
the aphrodisiac smell of your lips, parted,
slippery with spittle after many kisses.
Body that I praise because it is yours;
refuge I found out of my own abysses
after the trip had lasted many years.
Miracle that happened by accident,
golden palace where a nightingale lives,
sifting softly down through ivory leaves
phrases of music, each one different.

Writers in the Rain

This pluvial weather, power failures start.
With trainlines flooded, offices stay closed.
Who'll mend my dead computer in the dark?
After a while you come here in white clothes.
Later you leave once more. I nurse my hurt.
We sleep in different houses, but by night
the power flows back into my hand, inert
too many days, and forces it to write.

How many other seasons we have known
turn and depart, while we hid what we had.
The road that we have taken can't be seen,
and still our feet leave imprints on that road.
But now my sixtieth year comes on to me,
and cannot tell me by which roads it came.
In the wilderness of the world I tried to see.
If my spectacles were blurred, I am to blame.

The good that I pursued and hoped to find
comes to me even in the scent you wear.
Your lassitudes contain my promised land.
How should we answer for the way we are
in this strange love affair? I hear you smile
as your voice reaches mine across the rain.
'A mobile phone's some use once in a while.
Where will you be at twelve? I'll pick you up.'

Time in its ebbtide shapes new types of pain.
The aged computer that one feeds may stop.
If I turn round to praise the whiteclad branch
which is your body, down the slopes behind,
pulverous in thunder, comes the avalanche.
You offered me free passage to your mind.
No matter where I was, you were my home.
If time is short now, what we had still stays.

In the new century, when new people come,
they will know who you are, and offer praise
for beauty still retained, for skills honed true.
But you'll be guileless as when we first met
and will not understand what you should do.
Smile till they leave; then stay at home, alone.
Look through my tattered letters, if it's wet.
Once in a while, try out your mobile phone.

Alexander

Have they finally left, the mystic and mythic
powers I possessed? said their goodbyes?
I mumble in sleep, call after those absences,
though I know replies will not be made.
For whoever is very lonely and travels far,
at the end of the day, stumbles. Then it goes.
When my army flashed its shields over horizons
it followed my words, under perpetual snows,
eternal and vast ranges, strange stars, cyclic fires;
Over us always, circling, the carrion crows.

Write, scribe. I was my army. The world was mine.
exiled from two countries I hated and loved,
at the end of the day I was my own enemy.
But, scribe, write: at the end of it I had lived
a life so crowded others envied it; also
my path would not have been gladly chosen
by most. Look at me. I am my own ghost.

Twisted passes, fierce tribes. Steel scraped on steel
made sparks fly, harmless, but I flinched and winced.
Bloodfall I did not fear, only that sound
from childhood, chalks on blackboards. Still,
to the cringing Indians I have become Iskander.
With all my fears, unschooled, sorrow is known
better to me than most. Tomorrow now means little.

Scribe, at the end of the day came more betrayals.
By a deep river we broke the Punjab king.
Dragged to my feet, he wept, swearing his faith.
I needed love. I made him my brother. At nightfall
he came with swords behind us, killing my people.
An unfaithful and treacherous race. The end of the day.

Still I forded that river, entered that country.
The river was all I had come for, it waited for me.
It ran deep and still, I waded its waters.
Glycerine clear, they smelt of our Greek honey.
Had I held by them, they would have healed me.

But my body failed. I left the river, and then
barbarous men pillaged its shores for pleasure.
Write that down. I have no shelter from the sun,
where I lie, slowly dying in the city named after me,
for I left the river, went home over desert and sea.

Do not think that I am lonely. I retain some memories.
But I hear across distance that by my river
mothers tell children, 'Sleep or Iskander will kill you.'
I was never like that, scribe. The river could tell you.

Write that down, also.

Minotaur

Devil and saint in me. A crown of horns
cramps my skull. Bullsblood pumps my heart.
I grow away from grief. I read the runes
scribbled on cavewalls to foretell my fate.
My mother locked me in this labyrinth.
My father looms upon the public square
built over it. Bronzefleshed upon his plinth,
he stamps me down to where dead people are.

He will not save me, for he's not my sire,
Minos of the bitten beard and fretful voice.
I have no choice but to ride out my nightmare.
I know, concerning me, he had no choice.
The cow was wooden, but the queen inside
wasn't. She squirmed her buttocks at each thrust
from the gargantuan bull, the monstrous load
borne on her back in servitude to lust.

The monstrous load borne in her belly swelled
and became me, manshaped and still not man.
The mothersmilk that from her paps I swilled
filled up my bitter cup. Her breasts began
not to hide hate each day for many days.
Many years now since Pasiphai saw me.
I range and bellow in the keyless maze,
trying to find the face that is the key.

The gate to me must open from outside.
Nobody's seen me, or knows what I am,
except my mother, who I think is dead.
I have no mirror here, don't know my name,
and in my age I have grown animal.
Daily my eyeless keeper, through the gate,
nudges an uncooked corpse. This rancid meal
I gnaw and tear. Fullfed, I masturbate.

I have known no woman, only Pasiphai
and the imagined horde of whores who share
my little deaths. I watch them gasp and die
with me and, in their dying, disappear.
Gone far from grief, I find my shell alive,
thudded by heartbeats like a tribal drum.
Once the runes told me that I would survive
until the face that held the keys should come.

Shaped out of shadow, whiteclad, beautiful,
she comes to me. I hear the darkness stir.
Queenlike her features, and her body full,
and a great gentleness flows out of her.
An antique stench, putrescence, fungus, turds,
hangs in the labyrinth. She lowers her eyes.
Her outspread arms are like the wings of birds.
The face that looks down is not Pasiphai's.

In Cinnamon Shade

Now it is true darkness, the moon absent.
Churned by wind, clouds obscure the city.
Its walls, undermined by snails, collapse.
Shawled bats arrive, claim what remains.
Infestations of darkness destroy my words
and if the conclusion of darkness is dawn
I should know it, having watched the suns
rise slowly, set quickly, in many places.

But I turn on my side, my left hand lifted,
curved downward to cup a breast not there.
The cinnamon smell of the air around you
absent also. And the horned moon returns,
revealed by curdled and discoloured clouds.
How shall my great desire find your face
a second time, with the moon my enemy?
In the end only darkness, and I am tired.

Because of the moon, you have left my side,
for the moon made you different and afraid.
But wherever you are, I imagine you still,
sedated into sleep, long eyelashes sealed,
moist lips bereft. Rest in cinnamon shade.
Deep tides of darkness will cover the wound.
But of two once made one, what will be left?
Only footprints on water, handmarks on wind.

Rattlesnake

Morning opens its mouth. A firewind
scalds its way through the silences.

Whorled in its wound, a rattlesnake
ripples down the canyon under cactus.

Darknippled, heavy, ripened by sun.
your breasts taste of lost orchards.

The extinct volcano, maned with snow,
rears over you but will roar no more.

★

Quetzalcoatl will not come back
from the black abysses of hornets.

To the deep river which has no name,
you, dressed for sleep, will return.

Weep in white by white water, white
orchids of the forest surround you.

From glimpses in mirrors I inhale
and absorb your echo and your shadow.

★

Thorns clatter. The rattlesnake dies.
The time of the condor has not come.

Light falls level on empty altars.
Here a donkey's skull, there a child's.

Whiteclad you walk in leafless orchards.
Bronze orchids, your hands brush my lips.

Wet-eyed, one of the sun's trophies,
you enter absence and distance, lost love.